D0714212

MOTHERS WORK!

80003372993

MOTHERS WORK!

HOW TO GET A GRIP ON GUILT AND MAKE A SMOOTH RETURN TO WORK

JESSICA CHIVERS

HAY HOUSE

Australia • Canada • Hong Kong • India
South Africa • United Kingdom • United States

First published and distributed in the United Kingdom by:
Hay House UK Ltd, 292B Kensal Rd, London W10 5BE.
Tel.: (44) 20 8962 1230; Fax: (44) 20 8962 1239. www.hayhouse.co.uk

Published and distributed in the United States of America by:
Hay House, Inc., PO Box 5100, Carlsbad, CA 92018-5100. Tel.: (1) 760 431
7695 or (800) 654 5126; Fax: (1) 760 431 6948 or (800) 650 5115.
www.hayhouse.com

Published and distributed in Australia by:
Hay House Australia Ltd, 18/36 Ralph St, Alexandria NSW 2015.
Tel.: (61) 2 9669 4299; Fax: (61) 2 9669 4144. www.hayhouse.com.au

Published and distributed in the Republic of South Africa by:
Hay House SA (Pty), Ltd, PO Box 990, Witkoppen 2068.
Tel./Fax: (27) 11 467 8904. www.hayhouse.co.za

Published and distributed in India by:
Hay House Publishers India, Muskaan Complex, Plot No.3, B-2, Vasant Kunj,
New Delhi – 110 070. Tel.: (91) 11 4176 1620; Fax: (91) 11 4176 1630.
www.hayhouse.co.in

Distributed in Canada by:
Raincoast, 9050 Shaughnessy St, Vancouver, BC V6P 6E5.
Tel.: (1) 604 323 7100; Fax: (1) 604 323 2600

© Jessica Chivers, 2011

ISBN 978-1-84850-319-9

Printed and bound in Great Britain by
TJ International, Padstow, Cornwall.

For Nick, Monty and Artemis,
because I love you.

It is not weak to admit children affect work choices.

YVETTE COOPER,
MEMBER OF PARLIAMENT FOR NORMANTON,
PONTEFRACT, CASTLEFORD AND KNOTTINGLEY

Contents

Acknowledgements   *ix*

Foreword   *xi*

Introduction   *xiii*

Mantra #1   Know Your Ideal Work Scenario   1

Mantra #2   Keep in Touch and Ask for What You Want   49

Mantra #3   See Your Family as a Team   95

Mantra #4   Find Childcare that Fits Your Family   121

Mantra #5   Get a Grip on Guilt   157

Mantra #6   Go for 'Good Enough' at Home   185

Mantra #7   Prepare for a Smooth Return   209

Mantra #8   Do What It Takes to Thrive   235

Afterword   *267*

Further Reading and Resources   *269*

Index   *275*

Acknowledgements

First I must say thank you to all the people who shared their stories and experiences with me. Around 200 working parents completed the Mothers Work survey during the course of my writing, and thanks in particular to the mums who helped every time – you know who you are.

Many thanks to the extraordinary Karen Pine for encouragement and enthusiasm at every turn; your friendship means the world to me. My thanks also to the magnificent Allison Mitchell, Grace Lucas, Mathilde Murphy and Marie Loh for the various ways you've helped me on my journey – and of course all at Hay House.

Foreword

There is an incredible desire among mothers to return to work after children, yet the journey is not always straightforward or easy. There are many emotional and practical difficulties to overcome, not least the perennial question of how to manage both home and work successfully. I co-founded Women Like Us in 2005 because I knew many women needed support in finding quality the part-time work that would enable them to do just that.

In writing *Mothers Work!*, Jessica Chivers has echoed the need for women to receive more support as they transition back into the workplace – whether this is into full-time or part-time work. With a business background, many years of coaching women in career transition and her own experiences of being a working mother, Jessica is well placed to guide women through the process of making a smooth return to work.

What makes *Mothers Work!* such a good read is the voice of so many other women. It includes hundreds of stories of other mothers who have 'been through it'.

Karen Mattison, Co-Founder of Women Like Us
www.womenlikeus.org.uk
February 2011

Introduction

My decision to write *Mothers Work!* sprang from a comment by a mum I was coaching about feeling like she was in the wilderness before she went back to work. In her words, 'After postnatal classes the help seems to dry up and you're on your own.'

In an ideal world all women would have access to quality return-to-work programmes irrespective of how much they earn and whom they work for. I know there are some fantastic employers out there who offer the right support at the right time to their employees, but the sad fact remains that the majority of mums muddle their way back to work after children, alone.

Whilst I love to coach mums through the transition from working woman to mother to working parent, there's a limit to how many people I'll ever be able to help through 'comeback' workshops and one-to-one coaching, so the idea for the book was born.

I started writing with the single-minded aim of getting *Mothers Work!* into the hands of the mums who needed it as soon as I could. I was determined from the start to see this work in print even if that meant self-publishing. Thankfully, the first publisher's door I knocked on opened and I was invited in.

Combining work and a young family is not for everyone. Some do it because they want to, others because they have to. Others don't do it at all. This book is written with the intention of helping and inspiring the women who want or have to work whilst raising a family. You might be a first-time mum or returning to work after a second, third or fourth pregnancy. You may have had a big gap between the last time you worked and now, or be returning after a standard, single maternity leave. This book is for all of you, but especially the new mum who's finding her way for the first time.

It's my belief and experience – and that of many of the mums I know and have coached – that it's possible to combine work and parenthood in a satisfying and rewarding way. Working motherhood needn't turn you into the headless chicken-cum-wobbling jellyfish chimera some people would have you believe. However, maintaining your head and your backbone does, admittedly, require some skill. And that's what this book is all about: equipping you with the knowledge, mindset and confidence to keep your head and your family together.

Nearly 200 working parents have shared their stories, tips and insights with me by answering my Mothers Work survey. They have been very open and honest about what it takes to make working motherhood work. It's clear to me from all they've said, and from my own experiences, that the skills and techniques we need to survive and thrive can most definitely be learned. What I give to you in this book are what I call the 'Eight Working Mum's Mantras' – learn them, live by them and you're on the road to a smooth return.

Working Mum's Mantra #1: Know your ideal work scenario
Working Mum's Mantra #2: Keep in touch and ask for what you want
Working Mum's Mantra #3: See your family as a team
Working Mum's Mantra #4: Find childcare that fits your family
Working Mum's Mantra #5: Get a grip on guilt
Working Mum's Mantra #6: Go for 'good enough' at home
Working Mum's Mantra #7: Prepare for a smooth return
Working Mum's Mantra #8: Do what it takes to thrive

Each chapter explores one mantra in detail and is liberally splashed with comments from real working parents. The best advice I was given when I was pregnant was to listen to everyone and then make my own mind up. That's why I've included so many real working mothers' stories, to help you do the same. I encourage you to read everything with an open mind and take what is useful to you. Not everything will resonate with you, and if you don't disagree with some of the ideas here I won't have done my job as a thought-provoking coach and writer properly.

You'll also find a few exercises in every chapter, designed to help you figure out how you can usefully apply what you've read in your own life. I hope you will read and reflect on these even if you don't write anything down.

It's been said many times that it's a shame babies don't come with a manual. But thinking about it, if they did, wouldn't it need to be so big it would be impossible to read? In the same way I think there's a lot of stuff to say to help you as a working parent. Unfortunately (fortunately?) publishers give their authors word limits, so the tome I had in mind is now about a third of what I'd like to have given to you. As someone once wrote, 'I was going to write you a short letter but I didn't have time so I wrote you a long one instead.' With this in mind I pared down what I wanted to share, and give to you what I hope will be 65,000 of the most useful words to you on your journey towards working parenthood. Where I feel there's more to say, I've given you signposts to other resources.

Until being a working mother feels like business as usual, keep this book in your bag – you never know when you might need a boost.

Jessica
www.jessicachivers.com

MUM'S MANTRA

1

Know your ideal work scenario

**Considering your work options,
clarifying what you would like to do**

*Work may not be the most important thing in our lives or the
only thing. We may work because we must, but we still want
to love, to feel pride in, to respect ourselves for what we
do and to make a difference.*

SARA ANN FRIEDMAN

I spend a lot of time asking women what they want. Not because I am a Fairy Godmother with an idle magic wand (although, as for many of the women I listen to, there is definitely room for *her* in my life) but because I'm in the business of helping women get what they want. Knowing what a woman wants is kind of imperative if I'm going to help her get there, wherever 'there' may be. And if wands were there for the waving, what would you wish for when it came to harmonizing home, work and family? Would you work at all?

If your mind is in a fog and you haven't got clear answers to those questions, this book is for you. Knowing that you want to make a change is a good enough place to begin. And whilst this might sound a bit worthy, I'll say it anyway: my mission is to help you work out what you want for you and your family, and to support you in making it happen. I'm not a Fairy Godmother or Wonder Woman but I've been where you are now and I've talked to a heck of a lot of women who are doing a pretty good job of making working motherhood work.

According to a survey published in 2009 by the National Childbirth Trust, research by Liz Morris at Aston Business School showed that 61 per cent of mothers said they would work even if they did not need to financially, and nearly one in two said returning to work was as much about keeping their brain alive as anything else. Only 5 per cent said their ideal family scenario was for only their partner to work whilst they ran the home. Given you are reading this book, you are probably one of the 95 per cent of mothers who want to work in some capacity.

In this first chapter we are exploring the first of eight working mum's mantras: *Know your ideal work scenario*. Together we'll take a look at four different aspects of your ideal work scenario (because life's decisions are generally easier when we break them down):

1. **understanding your motivation for returning to work**

2. **deciding whether to return to your 'old' job or a new one**

3. **considering the hours you work and the way you organize them**

4. **the timing of your return to work.**

We'll delve into your ideas and preferences in each area and come up with a plan that suits you, your family and your colleagues/employer. In the next chapter we'll turn our attention to making your ideal work scenario happen by living the second mum's mantra: *Keep in touch and ask for what you want.*

Mums I've worked with say they find it really helpful to hear how other mothers do things – although admittedly we might not always follow the well-meaning advice we get given – which is why the whole of this book is intentionally *splashed*, never mind 'sprinkled', with the experiences, tips and reflections of women who've been where you are now.

'The financial pressures in society today make it difficult for most couples to depend on one salary. Therefore there is little choice

> *other than to return to work, which can make you feel guilty and out of control. However, when you have worked hard in a career it can be very refreshing to interact with adults and use the brain cells, other than talking about nappies and puke all day.'*

Over 200 generous souls (mothers, fathers, grandparents, aunts, childminders, employers, psychologists, nannies and nursery nurses) have shared their views, which I hope will help you get ready to make a confident comeback.

A friend once gave me a great piece of advice when I was pregnant with my first child: I should listen to everyone's stories and advice about pregnancy, birth and parenting, then work out what was right for me. I think she's absolutely right, and in the words of The Brand New Heavies, 'If you conceive it, you can achieve it' – so let the back-to-work journey begin!

HAVING IT ALL

Before we ponder your motivation for work, let's start with a bit of banter on the old 'have it all' debate. Yes, I know it's old hat, but still it rumbles on and I'd be a bland or wimpy kind of writer if I didn't have something to say about it. What do you think? What is 'all', and do you want it?

If I was being strategic it'd make sense for me to work out the least represented or most outrageous opinion so I could be wheeled out to take that stance on *Woman's Hour* or *Loose Women* next time it comes up. But actually, I don't have anything controversial to say about 'having it all' except that it sounds a bit greedy and stressful.

What I *do* think is a load of cobblers is all this talk of 'work-INSIDE-the-home-mothers' and 'work-OUTSIDE-the-home mothers'. I hadn't even heard this distinction until I started writing this book, and far from being a respectful way to acknowledge that all mothers work (and work hard), I think it builds barriers between mums. We're all in this together, remember.

> *'I can't see myself returning to full-time work; I'd feel too much of a swing the other way from the mundane to the insane. I don't think I could cope with trying to run a household, spend time with my children, have a strong marriage, do a good job, have a social life, etc. Life would be split too many ways for me. I thrive on doing things well and I just don't think I could maintain all of that at once.'*

When I hear the term 'working mother' I am *not* confused. I know it refers to a woman who has offspring and who does work additional to domestic stuff. It does not undermine in any way the women who choose to be mothers and not do additional work. Let me say it again so as to make it absolutely clear: ALL MOTHERS WORK HARD. It's just the things we work hard *at* that vary.

Any mother who does paid work for a significant part of her week cannot possibly do the same things to the same degree as a woman who does not do additional 'work outside the home'. And, of course, by having a 'job outside the home' you have added considerations and generally more things to think about in daily life than a woman who is more or less the same as you in every other respect but who doesn't have a paying job. 'Having it all' sounds a lot like perfectionism to me, and I know from my own experience, and those of all the women I've coached, that striving for perfection doesn't usually lead anywhere good. Which is why, throughout this book, I make reference to the idea that it's good to be good enough ('good enough' is, of course, open to individual interpretations).

'I feel there is tremendous pressure on women to return to work after having children and if you don't then many think you have "failed". I think it's a fallacy that women can have it all. Certainly they can have a career and a family, but I don't think you ever feel that you are doing either to the very best of your abilities – there are always compromises.'

Let's move on from having it all to having it the way we *want* it. Let's talk about reasons for going back to work.

YOUR MOTIVATION

Reflecting on my choice to take on an unpaid coaching project at the beginning of 2010, I posted a question on my blog about mothers' motivations to work. The replies show it's about so much more than money:

> **Karen**: One reason I work is to get feedback on my performance. When I was a stay-at-home mum nobody noticed if I'd reached my nappy-changing quota or fed high-quality food to my kids. There was no external affirmation; it all had to come from within. At work my performance was measurable, and noticed by others. I think feedback and appreciation are fundamental human needs, but small kids aren't in a position to give us it!

> **Lisa**: Too true, Karen! I have no clue if it is a male/female thing or a personality one, but so many of us have that overwhelming little voice shouting 'How am I doing?' Parenting in the early years can be a bit of a wilderness: everything that was clean gets dirty, everything that was full gets emptied, spooning it in one end and wiping off the other can leave you

feeling like you have made no mark on the world today. When you fast-forward the tiny increments of each day into a full year, you have obviously done the best job in the world, but, day to day, it can be hard to see the big picture. In the working world you either get it done or you don't but there is usually a direct and timely consequence: feedback – yay!

Sunita: I'm totally with both of you. I don't necessarily have to work for financial security, but I've worked so hard to become a psychologist that I want to pursue that. It is part of me, just like being a mum is. Plus my mum worked when we were kids and I never felt she loved me less or I was getting less of her. Feeling balanced is important to me; I am all these roles and my own person too. If the balance gets out of kilter I know I get anxious and stressed. Lisa is so right about seeing the bigger picture, too, as my two-year old seems to change each week and I don't want to miss that, so going to work helps me to prioritize the time so I don't put the washing before sitting and drawing with Lilly. Feedback is also important. I feel we should be our own friends and appreciate what we do rather than waiting for our partner or child to say what a great job we've done.

Jacquie: For me not coming back to work was not an option, as having done 20 years in the British Army I only need to do a further two for an immediate pension which is too great to turn down. The possibility of going to Iraq or Afghanistan and leaving the children behind for six months (possibly for life) is a worry and a fear words cannot portray. Still, looking at the here and now I can go to the toilet on my own and drink a cup of tea whilst it is still hot!

Tuesadaisy: With my older two children I was on my own, I worked for fear of being labelled a 'scrounging single parent'. Working allowed me some financial security and probably saved me from a very different life. Paying for childcarers, a childminder and then later a nanny brought me the family support that was missing, and gave my children some stability at a difficult time. In a new relationship with my third child I had the family support and the financial security to have the choice. At first I worked because I was frightened of spending whole days with three little people, but when my childcare arrangement broke down and I was forced temporarily into trying being a stay-at-home mum, I discovered that I quite enjoyed it. Not working became the viable economic choice for our family and I found I had to find my own space and well-being within the home.

Curious to know more about mother's motivations for returning to work, I asked over 150 working mothers about theirs. What they shared was illuminating – and perhaps most interesting of all were the answers to the question I posed at the end: *What top tip would you pass on to other working mums or those thinking about returning to work?* (Many of their answers are dotted throughout each chapter.)

Several women commented on their motivation for being a working mother. One mum cracked me up with 'Don't talk to mothers who are opting to be at home full time. They will make you feel like a witch!'

Health Benefits

Joking aside – this book is *not* about bashing stay-at-home mums – there are plenty of reasons why a woman would want to combine work with having a family. 'For my health' wasn't explicitly mentioned by any of the working mums I've talked to, but maybe you know already that education and employment are among the most important factors in closing the health gap between men and women?

Social psychologist Jason Schnittker has looked back on 30 years of trends in women's health, employment and family life and finds plenty of support for the health benefits of being a working mum. Here are three things you might be heartened to know (and that might assuage any guilt you feel) about working:

1. **Most studies show that employment (full- or part-time) improves and preserves health (e.g. see Ross and Mirowsky, 1995).**

2. **Household labour (as opposed to 'work outside the home') is associated with higher levels of psychological distress and less perceived control (e.g. see Bird and Ross, 1993).**

3. **Dual-earner couples are happier and healthier than their single-earner peers (Bartnett and Rivers, 1996).**

> *'It took a long time, but now I realize that I needed work to be happy. I am a better mummy for working.'*

While these messages are all positive, I'll say that Dr Schnittker's paper also reveals that some of the benefits of employment can be reduced if you're trying to work long hours *and* raise a young family. We'll talk more about this in a bit. For now, here are some more possible motivations for returning to work.

Money

Many mothers have no option but to work: their wages pay part, if not all, of the mortgage, put sandwiches in lunchboxes and bog-roll in the bathroom. In the UK a third of mothers with pre-school children work full-time (British Household Panel Survey or 'BHPS', 1994-2004).

> *'Not working radically shifted our relationship, because staying at home as mother and housewife is not "valued" as work even though it is really hard. Having some independent income is really worthwhile.'*

Even women who don't have to work out of financial necessity say having their own money is a powerful motivator for working. Co-author of *Sheconomics* Professor Karen Pine has this to say on the subject:

Even women who have no financial pressure to work tell us that earning their own money bolsters their self-esteem. Many find it demeaning to have to grovel to their husbands for money for personal items, such as make-up or clothes, if they haven't got their own earned income. Having a pot of money that's labelled her own makes a woman feel more entitled to dip into it, guilt-free and without having to consult anyone else. Most women who go back to work cite having their own income as one of the greatest benefits.

And what Karen says has rung true for women for a couple of generations at least. Here's Rosalind, a mum from the 1950s, writing to the Radio Four programme *Woman's Hour*:

And how invigorating it was to belong to the fraternity of working women, acting and paid! However happily married one is – and I can truthfully say I am – it is very depressing to be a head cook and bottle-washer, acting unpaid. Our husbands do their best for us, but how many of us ever buy anything for ourselves without feeling guilty, thinking that really the money should be buying tomorrow's dinner, or something for the home that is very much needed.

Mothers and guilt, will it ever end? Rosalind goes on to say:

Being a part-time office worker really has made a new woman of me. I don't say that I don't sometimes wish life wasn't so hectic, or that I never get tired or crotchety, but in the main I am better for it.

> *'It's tough being a mum and we often feel undervalued, but work isn't everything so you must either love your job or need the money to make it work for you – or consider a career change that can be more flexible.'*

IDENTITY

Mrs Incredible from *The Incredibles* warns her kids, 'Your identity is your most valuable possession. Protect it.' Jenny P, a management consultant who works two days a week, can relate to that:

Working gives me time to be 'me' – the 'me' I was before children – and I think it's important (for me at least) to remember that I wasn't always a mum and had a full life before being a mum. I also work to keep my professional life going. I love being with my kids and really enjoyed both maternity leaves, but I also love my job and spent a long time training to get where I am. I know that it is almost impossible to find a good part-time job – much harder than going from a full-time post to a part-time post with the same employer – and I really did not want to give up work for a few years only to find that I had to go back in right at the bottom.

How does Jenny's reflection on work and identity compare with your own? Does work matter? If not, what feeds your sense of self? If, like Jenny, work *is* an integral part of your identity, you might find it interesting to think a bit deeper about what work would be 'sufficient' for you to retain your identity but still allow room for the other important stuff in your life.

> 'Even though it won't add much to the family coffers once nursery fees are taken into account, my job keeps me sane and gives me a sense of identity.'

Can you happily maintain your sense of self working three days a week, or does it have to be five? If you're in a job that doesn't square easily with part-time status (and that's what you'd prefer), how could you potentially keep doing the aspects of the job you like the most without having to do it full-time? In the next chapter there's an example of a full-time solicitor who switched to two days a week, tweaked her job (to fit into part-time hours in a way that didn't compromise her identity) and still has time to be the mother she wants to be. Oh gosh, that's sounding like perfectionism, isn't it? The point is, our sense of self evolves and we don't necessarily need to work in the same way or at the same thing as we did before children, in order to feel good about ourselves professionally or full stop.

> *'Why did I go back? After baby #1: I loved my job. I took six months and I really missed work. After baby #2: at first it was financial reasons and the fact that I just couldn't cope with being a full-time mum. A year later ... I really enjoy my job, which is the reason I get out of bed each morning, but I go to work for a respite!'*

Freedom

Part of work for me has always been about freedom and having 'legitimate' time away from the children. I don't need to harp on about thinking they are the best thing since Dyson vacuum cleaners (they are), or loving my work (I do), but even if I didn't love my work I'd still want to get away from my kids several times a week. I literally skipped down the road the first time I left Monty, our eldest, with the childminder. Two-and-a-half hours of freedom, whoopee! You should have seen the smile on my face as I danced back to my home office; I was giving the Cheshire cat a run for his money. I was elated to be on my own and away from the constant cravings of my son. Do you know where I'm coming from? Is that part of work for you?

> *'Work for enjoyment and to fulfil your own needs, not others.'*

Kate agrees:

> If I'm absolutely honest I find small children (i.e. the under-fours) exhausting and, dare I say it, not that interesting (how about that as a comment for breaking a taboo?!). Older ones are fascinating – if I could have my way, we'd be able to access maternity leave when

kids are older – my 12-year-old needs me more than my two-year-old at the moment, yet I can't take leave to spend time with him.

Mental Stimulation

Photographer Hayley adds this to the mix:

> Although I love being a mum it was vital to me that I also did something else. I suppose if you work full-time and have a very busy work life it is healthy to have outside interests, and if you want your relationship with someone to remain strong it is a good idea to socialize with others. It felt the same being a mother.

And psychologist Sunita adds:

> I wanted to go back to work to be able to use my brain, gain a sense of self back, have more money coming in and also to allow Lilly to meet/get used to being around other children in preparation for school. I felt that she would be around a happier mother if I worked.

Writer Grace has also given this some thought:

> Finances play a big part in things but I think it has to be about more than this. For me, it's to reclaim some part of me that existed before the children. It's about giving another part of my brain a workout. I hope it will also make me a better mother from having a balance in my life.

Julia speaks to the team-player in all of us:

> At work you become part of a team and almost a community in which you all have a valuable contribution to make. There is a real sense of purpose and, particularly within support, a sense of achievement when you turn an unhappy customer with issues into a satisfied happy customer. This often has to be done very quickly, which keeps me on my toes! We also have constant challenges to keep our total support issues down and to work within Service Level Agreements, which can be frustrating but also drives you to do your best. Keeping my brain mentally challenged is also important to me, and the nature of support work enables me to do that, managing issue after issue.
>
> When on maternity leave, although I found a community of other mums, I missed the mental challenges and also the sense of achievement I get at work. It is also hard to explain but I also missed the whole atmosphere and buzz of being in a busy office environment.
>
> As a result of working I do find that the days and mornings off work when I'm with my daughter are more valuable and special, too. I think we learn to appreciate one another more.

Keeping Skills Up to Date

Mothers who've spent years studying, training and gaining experiences to reach the level they got to pre-baby say going back to work (even if they might prefer to take a longer leave) is about keeping themselves polished and marketable. 'There's no way I'm falling off the ladder just because I've had a baby' and 'If I don't go back it may be too difficult to pick up later on – things move on and I won't be taken seriously' are some of the comments I've heard women say. They don't necessarily feel a personal desperation to get back to work to polish those skills, but fear the consequences if they don't.

Researchers Sara Connolly and Mary Gregory have spent years exploring what happens to women's careers and pay trajectories when they 'downgrade' occupational status and hours worked. It doesn't make for pretty reading. In a paper published in 2009, Connolly and Gregory report that around 25 per cent of women in high-skill jobs downgrade occupationally on switching to part-time work, rising to 43 per cent among those who also change employer. Even when they return to full-time work and reverse the occupational downgrading there is only a partial recovery in earnings. Some 5.7 million women now work part-time in the UK, and the increase in part-time work has been particularly high in women in their mid-twenties to early forties (around 65 per cent of UK women work part-time at some stage in their adult careers, largely to enable them to better combine work and caring roles) so it's not so much the 'gender pay gap' that we should be worried about as the 'family gap' or 'motherhood pay penalty'. To quote from their paper:

While women in full-time work have been closing the gender pay gap through their rising educational attainment, labour market attachment and occupational diversity, women working part-time have conspicuously failed to match this progress. In 1975 average hourly earnings of women working part-time were 84.6 per cent of the earnings of women in full-time work, a pay gap of 15 per cent; by 1985 this had widened to 21 per cent, in the early 1990s to 25 per cent, and in 2001 to 29 per cent – one of the widest gaps among the advanced economies.

Critics of my interest in the financial status of mothers who work may say 'but money isn't everything' or 'it's more important for me to be able to care for my kids than earn what I did before' but that's beside the point. There is no reason why women shouldn't be able to maintain occupational status and the same pro-rata earnings when they switch to part-time work. The pay-penalty of part-time work does not have to exist, and I'm certain it wouldn't exist if men were suddenly asked to combine work and caring in the numbers women are. (I eagerly await statistics on how many fathers take up the right to share their partner's maternity leave and how much of it). I'll climb off my soap box now and let Kimberley, who works as a teacher, take up the reins with 'being a role model' as one of mothers' motivations for getting back to work.

Role Models

I sometimes ask my students (it's a boys' independent school 11–18) about their mums and whether they worked or not when they were growing up and the impact it had on them. The typical answer is, 'Mum's something in finance but she didn't work at all when we were little, she was there all the time until I was about eight ... oh, no, actually now I come to think about it we did have a nanny when my sister was little so she must have worked then. Hold on, I'll check.'

(Texts mum) 'Yes, she went back to work when I was two apparently and we always had a nanny. I didn't know that!' So as you can see it has very little impact on them! Another very typical answer is 'My dad is a manager and my mum just does a bit of work part-time in a nursery school but then my dad is much cleverer than my mum.' On further investigation it nearly always turns out that their mums have Cambridge degrees! So this for me is another reason for me to work. When my boys are older I want them to be proud of me, and if I had a daughter I would see it as even more important as I wouldn't want her to think that she could only have a career span that lasts until she is 30.

> 'Relax and try going back to work. You can always go home again (finances permitting) if it doesn't work out. Remember, if you don't value yourself your children will not learn to value themselves!'

Lawyer, Sarah C:

Having trained for many years and really fought hard to succeed in an extremely tough and competitive work-place, there was an element of feeling like I would be 'giving up' if I didn't go back. My mum was and still is the ultimate dynamic woman. She worked full-time with two kids and did a master's degree (she always made home-cooked food and we only had a cleaner when we were older) so I felt there was a lot to live up to.

To Contribute More Broadly

Psychologists have said that contributing to something bigger than ourselves plays a part in our perceptions of personal happiness. Some of the mums I've talked to (including one in the British Army and another who's worked for the RAF) say they work not just for the rewards it brings them but because of this sense of contributing more broadly to the world. There are the obvious roles like teachers, nurses, doctors, paramedics but also so many more jobs where women feel their contribution is really important, and that's part of their motivation for returning to work after having a baby.

> *'I felt I needed to do something that wasn't revolving around the children, plus I had set up my own business four years before I had my first child and I wanted to see that continue to flourish.'*

What are your motivations to get back in the workplace? Just think about them for a moment. Knowing *why* you want to work can help you shape your working life to be as satisfying as possible.

Exercise
My Feelings about Work

These four questions may sound repetitive but each one does get you thinking a little bit differently. They help you get a rounded view of your feelings and beliefs about working. If you're undecided about whether or not to return, or in what capacity, these questions might help you get closer to an answer. When I use this '2 x 2' questioning on myself (usually to get clear on something I'm hazy or being indecisive about) it always sharpens my focus and gets me to a decision. You might be surprised by your answers or they might confirm what you were already thinking. Clients I've done this style of self-reflection with have said it's thrown up things they hadn't consciously acknowledged were bothering them so that they can now do something about them.

How would I feel if I went back to work?	How wouldn't I feel if I went back to work?
Alive! Like a complete person. Happy, *guilty* too. Satisfied. Busy. Important and valued, true to my word about coming back after baby!	Unappreciated, frumpy, frustrated. Like I was getting nowhere. That my life wasn't progressing. I wouldn't feel boring and that I don't have something to say.
How would I feel if I didn't go back to work?	**How wouldn't I feel if I didn't go back to work?**
A bit relieved, but probably not for long. Relieved that I didn't have to try and do everything I did before. Less pressurized but frustrated that I didn't have my own money. Concerned about how I will get back to work when the kids are older – would I have the confidence and the skills?	I wouldn't feel the sense of achievement I know I get from working. I wouldn't feel stressed at the end of the day??? I wouldn't feel part of something, like a valued member of a team whose contribution is recognized.

DOING WHAT'S RIGHT FOR YOU

When I asked the mothers I surveyed for a 'top tip' to pass on to women preparing to go back to work, many of them talked about 'doing what is right for you' or statements along similar lines. They were very insistent on a woman's right to choose, and to sum up, their message is: every woman is different, every family is different and every woman's work circumstances are different, so cut the comparisons to avoid the guilt.

> *'It's very hard not to get swayed by other mothers, especially those who are not completely satisfied with their life choices and force judgements on your decisions.'*

To save your sanity and make things work, it really is important that you tune in to what works for you and your family. It won't be the same for the woman at work who returned from maternity leave just before you, or your best friend or friends from your antenatal classes. There may be people in your life who have tended to share the same ideals, beliefs or values as you but don't mirror your feelings about being a working mother. This shouldn't put you off doing what's right for you even if it's at odds with their views.

> *'Try and find a job that meets what you want out of it. Listen to your gut – all mothers are different and you will know in your gut what is right for you.'*

The people we spend a lot of time around can have a big impact on our attitude and behaviour as they are part of our 'psychological environment'. Beware of being overly swayed by well-meaning friends whose views on parenting differ from your own. I think antenatal classes are great and I've made some good friends from doing NCT and NHS classes, but it's worth remembering that initially you only spend time with the people you meet there because you happen to be having a baby at the same time. It's random chance who's in your group and whom you end up spending a lot of time around. If you were decorating your living room and standing in the queue with seven other people buying paint you wouldn't feel bad or wrong or that you had to justify your plans for painting your walls puce while they had chosen magnolia. In the same way you don't have to justify yourself or feel guilty or embarrassed if your ideas about how you want to combine work and family life differ from those of your friends.

What might your 'ideal scenario' be? Give yourself a moment to mull it over without reference to what other mothers do. Remember, their choices are irrelevant. How close is your ideal scenario to the realistic scenario?

> *'Resist pressure from external sources and be honest about what you want for yourself and what you can afford.'*

Sarah knows what it's like to compromise on some aspects of work to get closer to her ideal:

I made the move to be an in-house lawyer from private practice a few years ago very much to achieve a better work/life balance. Although the work is of the same calibre and interest, the pay is less, but there is no way that I would be able to work part-time at a law firm the same way I can now. I think the most important thing is to prioritize what you want out of life. For me that was my family and I was willing to sacrifice being a partner in a law firm for that.

SELF-EMPLOYMENT

I know first-hand that self-employment often gives us the flexibility we crave as mothers. It also comes with other stresses and strains, though, so it's not necessarily an easy option – especially if your self-employment also means a change in your line of work. Being one of life's planners I went self-employed as a coach and writer two years before I had my son, anticipating that it would be 'better' to combine

work and parenthood this way (I was kind of right and kind
of wrong). I also needed to liberate my soul from the corporate machine I worked for, and could not stand the thought
of staying with an organization just for the sake of the generous maternity benefits I would have got.

Is self-employment something you have thought of?
Could it work for you in your present line of work?

Mary, a PR consultant, made the move to self-employment when kids came along:

> I very nearly have my ideal work scenario. I work for
> myself and can set my hours so I don't miss vital
> school plays! I can also leave if one of my children
> is sent home poorly. The only downside to my work
> scenario is that, as I am self-employed, if I don't work I
> don't get paid, so the drawback is making up lost time
> in the evenings and weekends.

If you're thinking about self-employment or starting a business, act on these five golden nuggets:

1. Think through how much your time is worth and whether
    you can sell your goods or services at a high enough price to
    make it worth leaving your current job. Find out what other
    people charge for what you're planning to do and consider
    how you'll compete. Your local enterprise agency can help
    you with stats and data.

2. Turning a dream into a business is a great idea, so long as
    you can make it profitable. Preparing a business plan (see
    www.startups.co.uk) will help you work through the costs
    involved and other aspects of setting up to see whether
    it's viable. I can't stress enough how important this is, and
    many businesses stop here before they've started. My hus-

band and I got to this stage with plans for a high-end chocolate shop in the town where we live and realized we were far
better off all round if my husband stayed as an IT consultant.

3. Read about and listen to other business minds as much as
   you can before you take the plunge. It'll help you prepare
   for what's ahead, and other people's stories might help you
   avoid potential start-up problems as well as being a source
   of inspiration. For example *Making It* by Lou Gimson and
   Allison Mitchell will help you work out if you've got what it
   takes to succeed, as will hearing entrepreneurs talk about
   starting up: see www.sybmagazine.com.

4. Try and imagine how you'll feel doing something you feel
   passionately about as an idea or a hobby five (or maybe
   more) days a week. Are you really that into it? Or do you
   love it so much because it's escapism from whatever you do
   at the moment to pay the bills?

5. Think through the practicalities of where you'll work, where
   you'll keep stock or materials, how customers will do business with you and what childcare you'll need to make it
   work. Something I've learned is that kids and computers
   don't mix (I worked that one out the day Monty gave my
   laptop a drink, and I'm forever breaking my own rule of not
   working while the kids are around).

> *'I went back to the job I had and made some minor adjustments
> to make it work in a shorter period of time. This is what I am
> trained to do. I probably don't have any other job options without
> a lot of extra work having to go into creating them.'*

YOUR OLD JOB OR A NEW ONE?

What do you think about going back to your current job versus finding something new? For many it's a no-brainer to
start afresh (like it was for Julie, who was made redundant)

or to go back (like it was for Sasha because of the financial penalties). Sasha says:

> I'd love to jack in my job because I'm petrified of going back to it. It's just too much pressure and most of the people I work with just don't understand what it's like to be a working mum. I can't afford not to work and I can't afford not to go back to this particular job as I'd have to pay back some of the benefits I've had. I know though that it probably won't be as bad as I'm thinking now and I'm planning on looking for something new once I've done six months.

'I didn't realize I was looking for a job but was shocked into it as I realized a local company had just the right job for me – so I guess grab the opportunities that fall into your path and things will fall into place if it is the right step.'

More positively, Lee-Rose says:

> The main reasons for returning to the same job were – I like my job, I like the people I work with, the Council is flexible and they understand family situations. It's a very good working atmosphere and suits my current situation.

If it's not a straightforward decision for you, you might want to jot down the pros and cons of going back to something familiar versus starting afresh. One of the pros of returning to your current job is the 'firm-specific capital' you've built up in the time you've been there; that's valuable both financially and otherwise. In an analysis of 60,000 working women over a 27-year period, researchers have shown that if you want to move from full-time to part-time work it literally pays to stay in your current job. On average, around 25 per cent of women who move to part-time work 'downgrade' (occupationally and financially), but the extent of this downgrading falls to just 13 per cent when they remain with their current employer, compared to 43 per cent when they change employer.

One of the prominent reasons I've heard women mention for wanting to start afresh is to avoid comparing themselves – and being compared by others – to how they used to be before they had children. This is especially so if they believe they will not be able to do the long hours or work in quite the same way as they did before. Full-timer Vicky says:

I absolutely loved my previous job but I knew once Holly was born that there was no way I could go back because I couldn't keep up the long hours and crazy commuting. I'd set a level of expectation in my job about what I was prepared to do and on an emotional level I didn't want to let anyone down by not being able to continue with the lengths I went to before. I'm the main breadwinner and I've always loved my work so it was a no-brainer to return to work and starting with a new organization meant I could set my stall out and deliver on the new expectations I set. They know I'll always deliver but I'm home at 5.50 p.m. every day now and that's really important to me.

> 'My preference would be to go part-time, but I think even part-time working mums work like a full-timer. At the moment I am working full-time and it can be very difficult to juggle with being a mum, wife, etc. Prioritizing has made it better and kept me saner!'

On the flip side, many mothers feel it might be easier, more comfortable or just more enjoyable to go back to the same job, especially if they have a strong and supportive team around them and they enjoy their work. It is a highly personal choice and women usually advocate the route they have taken – if it has worked well for them – so it is probably a case of thinking through which route suits *you* best.

Alison says:

> Although it was a lot more work starting teaching at a brand new school, having to get to know new staff, children and parents, a new school layout and where all the resources were, I'm glad I did it. Since returning from maternity leave for a second time, I've found it a lot easier having been in the school for a year or so, and everyone's so supportive and understanding of you having a family. My new head teacher advocates a good work/life balance. I'm very lucky as it wasn't like that in my previous school at all, even though it's a very similar area and the two schools actually get comparable results! I've definitely learned what's important to do at work and what to let go of and not agonize over. Having a family has made me realize work's not the be all and end all, and if you're working for someone who makes you feel like that (whether you've got children or not), you need to get out of there!

> *'Weigh up the pros and cons of working part-time. You might end up doing a full-time job whatever part-time hours you are contracted to do.'*

PART-TIME OR FULL-TIME WORK

The majority of working mothers with young children work part-time. Some love it and say it's working well for them and their families, while others see it as a struggle they'd rather not endure. One full-timer I spoke to quit after six months to be a full-time stay-at-home mum (she says two parents working full-time was nigh on impossible without family close by. She said the end came when she realized they weren't having much of a life: spending whole weekends preparing meals for the week ahead being one of her examples). Another woman resents working full-time but does it because they need the money for the mortgage. An unusual example is the mother who works full-time for only part of the year – she is a contractor doing interim HR contracts for up to three months at a time. Although she's not full-time all the time, working this way can actually be much harder than regular full-time work because of the need for *extremely* flexible childcare. She also cites transitioning between being a stay-at-home mum and a full-time worker several times a year being a bit of a stress.

'I didn't want to leave the job market for fear of not being able to get back in at the same level. I didn't want to look for another part-time job as I know that finding a good one is not easy. At the end of the day my employer proved to be very flexible and supportive and I decided that I would be unlikely to find such a good employer providing good remuneration for doing really interesting work, so it made sense to stay!'

Full-time work has financial appeal but comes with many other non-financial costs, which is perhaps why so few of us do it. For some families there is no choice and it's not so much about financial appeal as financial *necessity*. At the time of writing *The Times* newspaper has recently reported that 20 per cent of wives earn more than their husbands, which is a five-fold increase on the 1970s and shows just how important women's employment has become to many families.

A survey of 4,000 mothers by Netmums in 2005 found that only 13 per cent of women on maternity leave intended to go back full-time, and of the women who were working full-time, only 12 per cent were happy. Of the full-timers, 50 per cent said they would rather be working part-time but needed the full-time salary, and 18 per cent said they couldn't find a suitable part-time job.

Positive Aspects of Full-time Work

Fewer than one in ten full-time working mothers being happy about their situation is a grim statistic. Given that full-time work is the reality for so many women, I'd like to reflect some of the positives:

- As mentioned, the full-time mother doesn't usually have to contemplate a downshift in work status and is more likely to be able to continue with the same responsibilities and rewards as she did before baby. Many part-time working parents cite this as a trade-off they made, for reduced hours and increased flexibility.

- You may love your work and feel fulfilled working full-time – a happy mother equals a happy home.

- There is often a pay gap between part-time and full-time work. The Netmums survey found the average rate of respondents' pay was £14/hour for full-timers and £11 for part-timers.

- There is without doubt a greater choice of roles available to women who opt for full-time work.

- It may be easier to move roles and/or employer if working full-time. Part-time workers can feel stuck in a job they'd like to move on from but the flexibility and good understanding they have built up with their employer are too good to give up. It can be a case of better the devil you know. As one mother says, 'I do think we need more "ready-made" part-time roles and employers will benefit from the loyalty of staff who are glad to have a good arrangement for their home life. It's sad that they should get that loyalty, really – I think many women feel trapped while working part-time, as they know they're not likely to find the same arrangements starting "cold" with a new employer.'

- Looking to the longer term, full-time work equates to a bigger pension provision even if full-time work doesn't give you much more money now than working part-time when costs of childcare and loss of tax credits are factored in.

The Part-time Work Story

Let me take you back to the work of social psychologist Dr Jason Schnittker and perhaps the most powerful reason why we would want to opt for part-time work over full-time work if possible. Dr Schnittker analysed 17,000 US parents' self-rated health scores and found that mothers working more than 50 hours a week reported poorer health than mothers working 1–30 hours, and that mothers working 1–30 hours reported better health than mothers who did not do paid work at all.

On the surface it seems that part-time work is the ideal scenario where our health is concerned. *However* (and this is a very big however), he also found that for women (not men – and I'll come to this in a moment) who have a child under six years of age, the more they work the worse they report their health to be. He stops short of saying that mothers at home with kids under six have better health than women who work, but that's the inference. I should add that the amount of income women were bringing in seems to lessen the problem somewhat, but not eradicate it entirely. Nor does the report dissect what is meant by 'health', and I suspect physical rather than mental health is what these parents are 'self-rating'. In this case, while it may be true that working parents with young children experience more physical symptoms of ill-health, I wonder how their mental health compares with non-workers? The majority of working women I've spoken to talk about the positive mental health benefits of going out to work, and many compare the alternative of being at home with the kids all day as a recipe for 'going ga-ga', 'mental', 'insane' – you know what I mean.

> 'Working part-time, I sometimes have days when I wish I was a full-time mum, but there are never days when I think I want to return to full-time work! That says something I think. Raising a child is so precious to me and the time goes so quickly that you really should enjoy every moment if you can.'

In 2009 US researchers Nancy Marshall and Allison Tracy published a study of the psychological health of over 700 working mothers. They had specifically examined the relationship between work and family characteristics and depressive symptoms, and found that, although working more hours was associated with greater work–family conflict, this greater conflict did not translate into greater depressive symptomatology.

'Be cheeky – even if the job advertisement doesn't say so, ask about part-time or flexible work. Especially for professional folk, if you have the skills, the employer may still be prepared to take you on board. I interviewed for one company in the UK who wanted to employ me despite part-time working, and have just got a job in the US part-time where NOBODY professional works part-time. Maybe it's just that I am usually not assertive enough about my abilities (I am led to believe this is a common female trait). Enjoy the professional journey while you have kids rather than worrying about your destination. I guess this is why it's called a "career".'

I'm going to get to dads and part-time work in a minute; forgive the circuitous route. I promise it will be worth it. First, I wanted to mention a woman who wrote me a passionate email about the apparent sexism in the title of this book:

I take it you are going to address the fact that the concept of your book is rather sexist. Mariella Frostrup apparently refuses to answer questions of the 'how do you juggle work and motherhood?' variety on the basis that no one asks her husband such questions, and in that I quite agree.

She may have a point and I like that Mariella is paving the way for parents to be seen as equals. However, it is naïve to pretend there is no difference between mothers and fathers, especially given that returning to work after children is usually a major life transition for women. It would be unusual for a father to feel this way, unless of course he has taken many months or years off work to raise his children.

A fine example of the difference between mothers and fathers is the finding, and I quote Dr Schnittker here, that:

> Fathers with children under 6 report better self-rated health if they work full-time rather than part-time. Indeed, fathers working more than 50 hours a week report somewhat better health than do fathers working 31–50 hours.

As several women have commented, they don't know how stay-at-home mothers do it because they see it as the harder option. Perhaps that's why longer hours worked by men equals better health, as it severely reduces the possibility that their partners call on them to be involved in domestic and 'childcare' duties too. Simply put, fathers working long hours avoid the so-called 'double-bind' of working mothers (working *and* doing everything else).

Part-time work is the most popular option for UK mothers. Here's a sample of their feelings about this:

- **Mary**, a PR Consultant who runs her own business: 'I couldn't entertain the idea of going back full-time (although the money was tempting) as I wanted to spend a lot of time with my children. I went back three days a week as, psychologically for me, that meant that I spent more days of the week with the children than I did without them!'

- **Hannah** works for one of the top 10 accountancy firms: 'I work four days a week. It's a pressure being a mum and it's good to get a balance that works for my career and gives me that extra time with my son. I feel like that day off is for me to make up for the nights I work late, etc. and is the one day I have just me and him to enjoy each other with no pressures to do anything/see anyone.'

- **Sam**, an HR manager: 'I work four days a week, but really am still doing a full-time job (if not more!). I have considered increasing my hours to take me back to full-time, just to get the work done. However, on reflection I realize that the work will always expand to fill the space, and instead I need to manage expectations and learn to say ''No'' (without feeling guilty).'

- **Carrie**, a project manager in financial systems: 'I've experienced both full-time and part-time work; once our son had started school I worked part-time (four days a week) to enable my daughter and me to spend time together, as I felt we'd not had that chance. It was lovely. When she started full-time school I returned to full-time work, but reduced hours again so I always take the children to school and pick them up. In truth I found part-time working hugely enjoyable from a selfish point of view, but it did make work more stressful so it wasn't unheard of for me to pop into work with a child (which they loved!), or work in my free time.'

- **Hayley**: 'Whether someone returns to work full-time or part-time for financial, emotional or other reasons is personal. I don't think any parent is wrong for choosing to be a full-time employee. For me, though, I would feel cheated of my son's and daughter's childhood if I weren't able to take part in their day-to-day lives, meet them from school every day or most days, etc. Part-time work enables me to feel like an individual while still being a hands-on mum. It's a balance and, for me, part-time makes it much easier to balance work and home life than full-time.'

- **Emma**, construction project manager: 'With my first child I had to go back to work ful-time when she was only 11 weeks old. I didn't like it at all and wish that things had been different. However with my second the plan was for me to stay off work, although I did do the odd freelance project to keep my hand in. Then when I had my third I was approached to go back to work on my terms when he was six months old, and by this time I'd had three-and-a-half years off. I decided to go back to work part-time; I felt this worked perfectly, and still does two years down the line.'

- **Mathilde**, information manager: 'Part time is great if you earn enough to cover whatever costs need to be covered. Work-wise, though, I found that three days part-time would not allow me to do all the work I had to (I did not have anybody to cover the other two days), so it is best to know how much you want, can and need to achieve in the amount of hours you decide to go back to. Children-wise, part-time allows me to spend quality time with my child when I am ready for it. I mean by this that after four days at work, I actually look forward to spending time with my son and can think of things to do with him. Staying at home all week, I have to admit I would run out of ideas *and* patience.'

The Struggle for Quality Part-time Work

Part-time work is the answer to many an organization's problem of a) not being able to find and retain experienced talent and b) not being able to afford a full-time member of staff to complete a particular part of the organization's activities. Yet, despite the obvious appeal, many parents (and non-parents who want more time for other aspects of their lives) are still struggling to find part-time work that makes best use of the skills and experiences they have. I get on my soap box frequently about this, and I'm not alone; as one woman puts the case on *The Times* Online's Alpha Mummy blog:

One thing I think is very important is the establishing of more good part-time roles and advertising them as such when people move on. It seems to me good business practice - you'd get lots of good applicants for many roles if they were offered up front as 3-4 days, and at the moment I think it's important that women do ask for days off if that's what they want to do, as it sets a precedent.

Often, part-time roles can make good sense because in many offices there are people who are overworked and someone needs to be there to pick up the extra work, but not every day.

I see job websites 'for mums' but they're all sales and franchise stuff, and not all mums have the outgoing and confident qualities you need for those, so I do think we need more 'ready-made' part-time roles and employers will benefit (as I hope mine have!) from the loyalty of staff who are glad to have a good arrangement for their home life.

It's sad that they should get that loyalty, really - I think many women feel trapped while working part-time, as they know they're not likely to find the same arrangements starting 'cold' with a new employer. It's lucky I like my job, as I could do with some more money, but I'm just not likely to find it without going full-time.

'I wanted to go back but I was keen to go back part-time rather than full-time. As this management role is a full-time job I proposed

doing a job-share in the role with another mum working part-time who had also previously done the job. However, my company felt this would not work and instead offered me a demotion, as team leader in one of the teams I had been managing. They told me I would maintain certain responsibilities to match my skills, such as appraisals and the monthly departmental statistical analysis, but I have not been able to do these as the new manager wanted to learn these himself.

'I do feel disappointed about this, as I am not fully using my skills. The team are great, though, and that does make a difference. However due to the marketplace and the fact I knew I would hopefully take maternity leave again after approximately a year, I didn't really see that I had any choice but to accept the position.'

In response to the 'part-time problem', Karen Mattison and Emma Stewart founded *Women Like Us* (www.womenlikeus. org), an award-winning social enterprise that helps women find work that fits in with their family commitments, through part-time job matching. Since its inception in 2005 Karen and Emma have matched, among others, lawyers, marketers, database managers, recruitment consultants and financial controllers to quality jobs that utilize their skills and experiences.

Emma Stewart, who also chairs the Family-friendly Hours Taskforce, says:

There is unprecedented demand in the UK from women with children who want to work, but who can only do so on a part-time basis. This creates a real opportunity for employers, particularly those who are struggling in the current climate, to access someone with, for example, £40,000 worth of talent, two and a half days a week, for £20,000. Part-time makes sense for families and for businesses.

This being a positive, proactive and practical kind of book, I asked Karen and Emma to make some suggestions for what women can do to help drive the agenda for better quality part-time roles in their own organizations. Karen says:

Reach while you climb. We need more successful women to open up about their experiences on their way to the top, and how they have managed to achieve a balance that works for them. The more we communicate this, the more that flexible working will become a part of our culture.

What about the wider picture in the UK? Well, it's getting brighter if the UK Government Equalities Office's 67-page document *Working towards equality: A framework for action* is anything to go by. Published in February 2010, it states that (a Labour government) is committed to '... creating a fair and family-friendly labour market where everyone has the opportunity to develop their skills and experience [and that it] is a necessity if we want our economy to return to sustained growth.'

Now, while that's not a guarantee of a greater number of better-quality part-time roles in the public sector (and bear in mind that Labour have now been replaced by the new coalition government), nor a threat that the Government will legislate to drive the private sector into doing the same (would we want that anyway?), it *is* encouraging to know that the 'part-time problem' has at least appeared on some-one's political agenda.

Thinking back to the research by Nancy Marshall and Allison Tracy, the Government should also be interested in driving the agenda for better-quality part-time jobs because their research found that (low) job quality is significantly associated with depressive symptoms in working mothers at both six and 15 months post-partum. In 2003 depression was estimated to cost the UK over £9 billion, of which £370 million was spent on direct treatment costs.

Let's follow the UK Government's actions with interest – and in the meantime what if all of us were to do what we can to stir things up for the greater good in the organizations and communities in which we work? Perhaps you are an employer? You could look at ways to integrate more part-time roles into your workplace. We can't wait around for others to make things happen. In the words of Anne Frank, 'Isn't it wonderful that none of us need wait a moment before starting to change the world.'

> 'With both my children I went back to work when they were four months old, as that was as much as my company could afford to have me off! Ideally I would have liked to have gone back to work when the babies were older, at least nine months old, as both times going back to work was incredibly hard when they were so young and I was still so exhausted!'

BACK TO WORK TIMING

In the UK, Statutory Maternity Pay/Maternity Allowance (SMP/MA) covers mothers for nine months and, naturally, many mums time their return to work to coincide with the end of it. It's at this point I'd like to state with some certainty the average length of maternity leave, and how many working mothers we have in the UK. Even more interesting would be how these statistics change according to whether a woman is mother to pre-school or school-age children. But the Office for National Statistics couldn't tell me, and I don't suppose they can keep tabs on everything. Although, just in case you're interested, they *do* know that softwood conifer production is likely to rise from an annual average of

6.9 million per m³ in the period 2007–2011, to 8.2 million m³ in 2012–2016. Somebody somewhere may be very keen to know this, but I suspect you are not that person.

> *'I went back when my son was 11 months old. The timing was good for me – I was ready to go back and fed up of not having 2 minutes to myself – although it was a tricky time for my son. He was in a difficult phase and the separation anxiety had just kicked in, and I still have the clingiest baby I have ever met nearly 10 months later. I would put a second baby in nursery earlier to be fairer to them.'*

Let's assume the majority of working mothers return to work when their babies are between six months and a year old. It may be more or less depending on your situation and how generous your organization is with additional maternity benefits. What's remarkable about this timing is that it coincides with the peaking of separation anxiety (widely quoted as occurring in the second half of the first year and lasting two to four months, although this is acknowledged to vary substantially) and instances of illnesses in early childhood, which peak at 12 months and then slowly decline (upper respiratory infections, ear infections and gastrointestinal infections are cited as peaking at 12 months by NICHD Early Child Care Research Network, 2001). Making a return at this time may be compounded with the distress and distraction of a child who doesn't want to be left in childcare or can't be left due to ill-health. However, and there's always a big HOWEVER when it comes to our kids because they do vary so much, there are so many factors to take into account when you return to work that you may not have a choice about the timing, and on the positive side your child will probably settle into his or her new routine absolutely fine.

Anecdotally speaking, my son started with his child-minder when he was five-and-a-half months old, and compared to a lot of his peers who started at day nurseries or childminders when they were several months older, Monty seemed to settle more quickly. This may have been down to natural variations in personality *or* to do with his having started with the childminder younger. It's only natural that the longer our children have been used to exclusive care from us, the more they might kick up when left somewhere new with people they don't know very well yet.

Jenny describes the impact of the difference in back-to-work timing with her two children:

> with my first child (Joseph – now four years old) I returned to work when he was seven-and-a-half months – this was a good time as he wasn't at the separation anxiety stage. With my second child (Harry – now nearly two) I returned to work when he was 11 months and it was a lot harder.

In the US, where there is no Statutory Maternity Pay, 56.4 per cent of mothers with children under a year old go out to work, and the majority of them return to work by the time their baby is three months old (US Department of Labor, 2008).

Coming at this from the perspective of living in a generous welfare state, you might think this is cold or unnatural, but founder of LifeWorkLife, Kirsten Hemingway, reckons it's much easier to go back when the kids are really small. She says she was breastfeeding in boardrooms and much more able to get on with her business when the kids were still babes in arms. She's clear that she thinks maternity leave is too much about the organization and not about the mother:

Ideally we'd all be free to return to work or dip into things as and when we feel ready. It's no wonder going back can feel like such a traumatic experience if you leave work and have very little involvement in the business for 12 months. It feels completely alien when you do go back, so why leave completely in the first place if you don't want to?

Kimberley also extols the benefit of sowing career seeds while still on 'official' maternity leave:

I started my master's degree when my second child was four months, and although it was tough it was so worth it. I did it part-time in the evenings so the actual time away from my children was very little but I was able to work in the evenings/when they were sleeping to do something intellectually stimulating and something that made me feel like me. It meant that when they were being difficult I could cope because I felt that I wasn't a slave to them or to domesticity but that I was still me, and this made me a much more contented and responsive mother. It also meant that I was still developing my career while on maternity leave, as I'm not sure I could have got the job I've just got without it.

For her part, Samantha says:

I recently returned to work, just before my daughter turned a year old. I was mentally ready to go back to work sooner, but was fortunate enough to be able to take the full year off, maximize the time with my daughter and enjoy the summer. Overall I'm enjoying being back at work, but I have good days and bad days. I work four days a week now, which I find gives me a good balance – enough time in the office to feel I can do my job, and enough time at home to do mum-and-daughter things.

Julie, a management accountant, feels that while there's no definitive 'right time' to return, we should make a decision and stick to it:

I went back at eight months with both my children, and I don't think that there is ever a perfect time, but I think once you make a decision about when to go back you should stick to it, as you can always say 'just another month' which can make it harder for everyone. I was ready to go back with my first, Adam, after eight months, but felt I could have stayed off longer once I had Eloise, and after being back at work for a month-and-a-half I am still not sure yet that being back is the right thing for me.

BUT I DON'T WANT TO GO BACK!

According to *What Women Want*, a report published by the UK Centre for Policy Studies in 2009, 31 per cent of mothers don't want to work. If it's a necessity that you return to work despite wanting to remain at home, here's how women who've felt like you have reconciled themselves to it.

One mum I surveyed suggests seeing going back to your job as a stepping stone to something you *do* want to do – in her case, self-employment:

I had the chance to change careers, which has been wonderful. It would've been much harder, though, if I'd gone straight from at-home mum to new career. I needed to return to my old job and regain my confidence before considering the job change.

Georgina:

I was keen not to go back to work but we'd decided to move to a better area for better schools and we just couldn't live without my earnings for the mortgage. During my coaching with Jessica I started to pay more attention to the upsides of going back to work, and this really helped me because I started to see going back as a positive choice. We could have moved away again but I didn't want that, so work was what I had to do.

Freddie:

I had to convince myself that working and bringing in money was providing a better life for my kids, and that in the long term they wouldn't remember if I was there or not. Plus I got a job where I could work most of the time from home, and had the kids looked after in the home, in an environment they were used to.

Fiona:

By being realistic and realizing that most of the other mums I knew from my baby group and the school playground were working, too, I felt better. Very few women these days have the luxury of being a full-time stay-at-home mum, and although I didn't really want to go back the quality of life is definitely better because I work.

Hayley:

I initially thought I *had* to go back, and when I returned to work for a pre-going-back interview I felt that it was totally wrong. I really didn't want to go back and felt quite ill at the thought of it. I talked to my husband that evening (who'd always assumed I just wanted to return to work — because I had led him to believe that) and we did some sums and worked out that I didn't have to. It was such a relief and I realized that it had been a burden for a long time thinking that I would have to return to the same job. I retrained in a completely different area of work because my previous job would not fit in with the children's education and out-of-school activities. I always knew I wanted to return to work, though, and was lucky enough to have the chance to change direction and retrain.

Many mums I surveyed echoed the idea that 'the thought of going back is worse than actually going back,' and other mothers implore you to stick at it because 'although it is a big wrench, you can get used to anything.'

KEY IDEAS & ACTION POINTS
The lesson for this chapter is 'Know your ideal work scenario.'

- **Motivation**: What's your motivation for going back to work? Be honest. Can you capture your feelings in a sentence? Being explicit about why you are returning to work can be helpful when making choices and decisions.

- **Old Job v New Job**: If you have the option of or potential for quality work at your current employer, the majority of mums would encourage you to stay.

- **Part-Time v Full-Time:** Part-time work is the most popular choice for mothers of young children. It comes with costs and benefits, as does full-time work. What's your preference? Thinking broadly, what would suit you and your family best at the moment? How can you achieve that?

- **Timing:** Make an informed decision and have a plan that's right for you. Many mothers say it's easier to go back before their children have entered the separation anxiety stage (the second half of your child's first year) or after the peak of childhood illnesses which is around 12 months.

- **Have to but don't want to go back?** My mums are clear: Distract yourself from the downsides and play up the positives. From all the life experiences you've had you can probably find a sliver of silver in the cloud.

MUM'S MANTRA

2

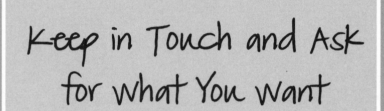

How to reawaken your confidence and ask for what you want at work

You can't ask for what you want unless you know what it is. First you have figure out what you want. Second, you have to decide that you deserve it. Third, you have to believe you can get it. And, fourth, you have to have the guts to ask for it.

BARBARA DE ANGELIS

Six months after Lou Gimson had her first baby (she now has three girls, is a single parent, businesswoman extraordinaire and sought-after speaker) she weighed up the pros and cons of returning to work. Like many of the women you read about in the first chapter, Lou needed to return to work for financial reasons but she also wanted to do it because her work was a key part of her identity.

At the time Lou returned to work she had a self-employment option but felt she needed to work within a team to get her pre-baby confidence back. 'Social contact with adults' was also an issue cited by more than a third of the women in The NCT/Liz Morris study (mentioned on page 3) as a reason for returning. Lou's ideal scenario was three days a week, term-time only. Thinking the situation through from her would-be-employers' perspective (a college), she posited her request for flexibility as a solution to a business problem they had overlooked – that's why she's a successful businesswoman in her own right, I guess! Lou's approach was to suggest that it wouldn't be worth their while paying her to be part of the college during holiday time when students are away, and instead wouldn't they prefer to save money and employ her on a freelance basis, term-time only? Putting it like this, the college said yes quicker than a toddler offered a chocolate biscuit *AND* a lollipop.

This chapter explores the second working mum's mantra for making going back to work, work: *Keep in touch and ask for what you want.* Like Lou, flexible working is probably a part of your ideal work scenario and something you would like to ask for. But before we start asking for anything, we need to get into a confident mindset.

DEVELOPING A CONFIDENT MINDSET

You've been away from 'work' for what probably seems like a lifetime. Well, you have – your baby's lifetime. And we both know you never stopped *working* anyway; you just traded one set of challenges for another. Whether it's been five months or 25 since your 'other work', you might be feeling unsure, worried or just a bit weird about returning to it. I know that's how I felt. Of course there's always the possibility you're brimming with positivity and confidence, which is marvellous. Hang on to the feeling and go for it.

> *'Perhaps it's just me, but I found being away from work for a year gave my confidence a huge knock. I had to give myself a big talking-to before I went back to work – if I was doing a great job before I had a child, why wouldn't I when I returned to work? It took a little time, but I soon got back into the swing of things and actually now feel like a more rounded "contributor" to the business.'*

As we heard earlier, founder of LifeWorkLife Kirsten Hemingway has what some might say is a radical approach to retaining professional confidence after becoming a mother: she advocates a move away from the traditional maternity leave.

It's so hard to go back, so why leave? I think maternity Leave is bad for women and I feel very strongly that it is arranged around the work not the person. I found it easier to work in the first six months after the birth of the children rather than after that when they were on their legs!

As we'll see later on, some women keep their hand in at work; maybe you have too? I didn't have a traditional maternity leave with either of my kids, although there were nine months between my last corporate coaching workshop and the first one after Monty was born. I felt worried and ridiculous before I coached that first time. I wondered how on Earth could people take me seriously when for the last few months this time of day saw me in baggy, liberally milk-stained pyjamas, wrestling to keep my recalcitrant infant on his changing mat and chanting new words to old nursery rhymes (for my own amusement, not his). In short, I thought I risked looking like a reality-show participant positioned deliberately out of her depth to make good TV and, once everyone had finished laughing, would be clearly labelled as an imposter. However, I settled into my groove and with a baffling mix of emotions – on the one hand proud of myself, on the other a little disappointed that something I'd feared so intensely was in fact a doddle. The experience taught me just how quickly we can feel comfy in old roles. The fact of the matter is there's no reason why you shouldn't be as good as you ever were.

> 'Believe in yourself even if you've been out of the workplace for some time; it doesn't invalidate your professional skills and experiences: they just lie dormant for a while, and it's amazing how quickly it all comes flooding back.'

YOU'RE STILL AS GOOD AS YOU EVER WERE

The thing is, disappointing as this might sound initially, people don't change very much. That's the picture built up from decades of observation and psychology research, at least. And that's a good thing, especially if you were good at what you were doing before you had your children. It's not to say you can't change or improve if you want to, just that change requires preparation and sustained effort – but that's a story for another book. (See *Changing for Good* by James Prochaska *et al.* if you're keen to overcome unwanted habits or sustain some good ones.)

> *'However confident you are about your abilities, it's still nerve-wracking going back to work, isn't it? In those 3 a.m. panic thoughts, you fret about everything from will you actually still be able to do the job – please God let there be some brain cells still sparking in your brain; will the person working your maternity cover have kept everything ticking over or – even worse – will she have been better than you, to cringing over the fact that you're still in elasticated waist trousers! I think we need to acknowledge that a confidence crisis and nerves are perfectly natural on your return to work. What helped me was telling myself that I'd done my job for a long time, I was (hopefully) good at it and there was no way that all that could have disappeared during my maternity leave. And, you know what, even when you don't FEEL confident at first – fake it! Pretty soon you'll be back up to speed, enjoying being part of a working team again and you won't have to fake it any more.'*

Just as you'll notice many of the same people queuing for the bus or on their regular spot at the station in the morning, so too will you get back into doing what you did before far more easily than you might think.

You may even surprise yourself with more refined organization or negotiating skills. Perhaps your patience will stretch further than it used to or your team will respond warmly to your new hands-off-and-let-them-learn approach. You've certainly become a consummate juggler, and it's not just the circus who'll pay for that.

It's been said before and it's worth saying again – particularly because it should give you an instant confidence boost: there are more parallels between motherhood and 'other work' than you might think. All the time you thought you were just getting through the day you were actually honing some of those much-hyped transferable skills. Coaxing your children to eat every mouthful, then cleaning the same old patch of floor after every meal without getting too cross shows persistence and the ability to deal with daily frustrations (not unlike dealing with bureaucracy). The way you broker deals with your pre-schooler about getting dressed and putting X number of toys away in exchange for 20 minutes of her favourite DVD paves the way for more assertive negotiation with your boss about things she delegates to you. The way you clean bottoms so caringly, and stop tantrums and tears with aplomb …

> 'In hindsight I'd worry less about how I'd cope. You've already learned to juggle from having a small baby to look after. Going back to work is just more juggling. You just have to get on with it and you'll be pleasantly surprised. It does all work out.'

While it's widely reported that women tend to experience a (usually temporary) loss of confidence about going back to the workplace, some mothers contradict that, saying motherhood brings its own confidence. Take Rebecca, a 30-something solicitor and mother of two:

whilst I did feel slightly nervous and apprehensive about my first day, I also felt I had renewed confidence, especially after returning to work after my second maternity leave. Having been at home for several months juggling the demands of two children under two, I felt that if I could cope with that I could deal with whatever work had to throw at me!

Developing a positive attitude like Rebecca is about recognizing and giving yourself due credit for the multitude of skills you are using every day to cope with the demands of young children. You needn't be consciously drawing parallels between your mothering skills and your professional life to benefit (although it's undeniably a neat way to boost self-esteem and rev yourself up for your return).

Let's turn now to a characteristic of confident women and the thrust of this chapter: being able to ask unequivocally for what you want.

Exercise
Motherhood–Work Parallels

Give yourself 10 minutes for this exercise and try doing it with some uplifting music in the background. 'You Are the Universe' by The Brand New Heavies and 'You Gotta Be' by Des'ree could give your confidence a boost.

If you are pushed for time perhaps think about it while you're feeding your little one, writing things down between spoonfuls.

- Divide a sheet of paper into two columns.

- On the left write down any skills you feel need polishing before you go back to work, e.g. assertiveness with boss, delegation, speaking up in meetings.

- Next, challenge yourself to think about situations you have faced since becoming a mother. Think how you've handled them and link them to the skill you want to improve.

- Write your thoughts in the right-hand column.

Come back to this tomorrow and see what else you can add.

THE PSYCHOLOGY OF ASKING FOR WHAT YOU WANT

Nice girls don't ask? It seems when it comes to negotiating a pay deal or accessing other work-related opportunities – such as flexible working – women and men do things differently. As a result, in the case of pay, women earn less. **Fact: if you don't ask, you don't get** – and what's so important about being nice? OK, there's a fair bit to be said for being nice, but being nice, working the way you want to work and earning a decent wage *can* co-exist.

'My old boss had the approach to the job of, "I don't care how you get there, as long as the work gets done." This meant that she could accommodate a wide variety of suggestions from the employee (for example, for one colleague with school-age children she was happy for her to leave early to pick them up, knowing that my colleague would put the kids to bed and carry on where she left off, making up her hours then). My boss was also a mother, and although she employed a nanny for her own children, she didn't expect you to follow her example. She respected your choice in childcare, and that it takes time for a

child to settle – and so I never felt inhibited discussing ways to help ease the transition in returning to work – for example she would have agreed to shorter days with a later start time for a period of time until my child was comfortable in a new setting. I really think that she understood that a happy mummy equals a focused and committed member of staff.

I have worked for other people who are not quite as imaginative to say the least! They have felt that you have to "clock in" and "clock out" at the set time, with an attitude of "well, that's how it's always been done" or "I don't want to set a precedent for others." Then there are the women who chose to return to work after three months and leave their children in nursery from 7.30 a.m.–6 p.m. In real life everyone is different, and just as you would respect their differing views on, say, religion and politics, an ideal employer should listen to your concerns and worries and try to offer solutions which could satisfy the needs of the business and those of the parent employee. Both can co-exist with a little imagination.'

Economics professor Linda Babcock is the inquisitive mind behind research that shows that American women working full-time earn about 77 per cent of men's salaries. Even when she factored in differing professions, education and other variables, women who had worked full-time and not taken time off to have children still experienced an 11 per cent pay gap. Babcock's study into gender pay inequalities began when female graduate students complained about male counterparts in the PhD programme teaching on their own whereas they were working only as teaching assistants. The explanation was simple: the blokes had asked to teach, the women had not. So the message is simple: ask for what you want and you might get it. Don't ask and you *certainly* won't.

When clients ask me to help them with perceived in-equalities at work I usually try and steer them away from comparisons with others and towards 'running their own race'. I ask what they want. I ask what matters, what they think they are worth, what they would ask for if they knew the answer would be yes? I encourage them to be proactive. The sad fact is that women tend more than men towards *reacting* to opportunities, rather than *creating* them. We're also less likely to strike out with a pitch to do something differently or to ask for a promotion or a pay rise unless we see someone else do it. I once read that when men look at a job specification they will apply if they can do 30 per cent of it, whereas women who can do 70 per cent will think they're insufficiently qualified.

Babcock's female graduate students were politely waiting to be asked if they'd like to teach, and that strategy clearly doesn't work in the workplace. Another study by Babcock and co-researchers Deborah Small and Michele Gelfand found that men are nine times more likely than women to ask for more money when offered a small payment for taking part in a game. In the experiment, men and women were asked to play four rounds of the word game Boggle, then the experimenters offered them three dollars, saying, 'Here's three dollars. Is three dollars OK?' If the participant asked for more money the experimenters gave them ten dollars. If they grumbled but did not make a direct request for more money, they were not given any more. There was no difference in how well the men and women rated their skill at the game, so it wasn't that the women weren't asking for more because they didn't think they played as well.

Let us learn from the Boggle study and galvanize ourselves to ask for the way of working, the pay and the conditions we want. We might not get them – and there may be good reason for that – but at least we've sown the seeds and got our organization thinking about what we need as working parents.

One mother and teacher I spoke to is a great example of a woman who saw the value of asking for part-time work and a pay rise in spite of the odds being stacked against her. In her own words:

I applied for my post as a Director of Subject (which is always a full-time post) but when enquiring stated I would only be able to do part-time. I sent my CV and full application and really did not expect to hear much more. They called me for an interview along with a strong field of people who were able to offer full-time.

At the interview I was asked about when I would be able to commit to full-time. I did not agree to anything for full-time and said I would need to see how my family needs were after a year or two. After seeing more of the department and the nature of the school I was convinced I would not be offered the post as it was a demanding role managing many people in a busy department. However, despite my conviction it transpired that the school were keen to employ me based on my previous experience, and along with some other negotiations I was offered the post. Teachers' pay is divided into two parts: 1) Main teaching pay and 2) Any management allowances. Since being in post and needing to put in many extra hours on the two days I am not in I have managed to negotiate that the management part of my pay is paid in full and the teaching part remains equivalent to the number of days I work.

Juggling this job part-time is very demanding but more than worth it to have time with my daughter while maintaining a job at the level at which I was working before having a child. I had never thought that posts advertised as full-time could be negotiable. I thought this only really happened if it was a job that had previously been yours before having children.

Allison is another example of a proactive teacher who set about removing the obstacles to working the way she wanted. And I'd like to offer a big round of applause at this point to all the teachers who model so many good behaviours for our children to learn from. You are a credit to the UK and don't get praised publicly nearly enough in my opinion. Returning to Allison, in her own words:

The head teacher I worked for when I returned to school after having Luke offered me either one day or five days - she couldn't understand that I didn't want to work full-time as I'd always been so committed to my job. I'd asked her if I could return to work part-time (for two days a week) nine months after having Luke, as our parents could cover our childcare for two days a week, very luckily for us. However, the Head wouldn't budge at all, saying she didn't like job-shares (even though she'd actually done a job-share on her return to work from maternity leave), so I ended up sending a letter round to the schools I wanted to work for in the local area asking for one day a week teaching work. Through a friend's contact, I ended up going into a local school for an informal interview/chat and the head teacher there offered me one-and-a-half days' teaching if I could persuade my previous head to give me just half a day. So I ended *up working half a day at my previous school and 1.5 days at the new one. Although it was a lot more effort starting teaching at a brand new school, having to get to know new staff, children and parents, a new school layout and the location of all the resources, I'm glad I did it as the new head's been so great and actually offered me the two days I'd been looking for originally after just a term's work.*

Allison's experience shows what a pivotal role our colleagues and contacts can play in helping us make a confident comeback. For Allison, asking her friends and their friends about opportunities (what you might call 'working your network') was what won her the work she wanted.

KEEPING IN TOUCH WITH COLLEAGUES

One of the things many mothers say helps them feel confident about going back to work is the contact they've had with their colleagues while they've been away. Especially as that contact can pave the way for easier conversations about various requests you might want to make.

When you're in the middle of your maternity leave you might not want to know the ins and outs of how various projects are progressing or anything else that would matter if you were in the thick of it, but contact with colleagues can be reassuring. As you journey towards the end of your leave you might be keen to know a bit more about what's happening to help you get ready to return.

> *'I popped into work with the baby and hoped like hell that she'd be well behaved! I also had a couple of colleagues come to see me at home to meet the baby and emailed, etc. to keep in touch – just with my team. I also went to the work Christmas do, which was useful.'*

As Lee-Rose says:

> I went into the office a few times, mainly for social visits. I didn't do any work and didn't want to know anything about work. I wanted to keep in touch with my colleagues so it didn't feel strange when I returned, but I didn't want to think about the work at all. It's good to keep in touch so that they don't forget who you are! I also set up a meeting the week before I returned with my Team Leader so that I could get the latest information on changes that had been happening within the department and also changes with work, as the project work had changed whilst I'd been off. This prepared me before going back and gave me an idea of the type of work I would be doing instead of going in blind.

KIT Days

Many organizations are excellent at keeping maternity leavers in the loop with changes and updates, whilst some seem to forget they still have a duty towards you as an employee. As a bare minimum your organization should keep you informed of organizational changes, vacancies and changes to policies and practices – just as they would communicate to regular employees.

If you *have* been in regular contact with your boss through KIT (Keep In Touch) days or informal channels, then making the call to discuss your return is probably straightforward. You might even have put a date in the diary to catch up, before you went away, or been proactive and jointly prepared a plan for your return to work.

It's worth mentioning that women who have KIT days tend to report a much easier transition back into their work than women who don't.

> 'KIT days are absolutely essential – they should be planned months in advance and never missed – once a week is good.'

WHAT ARE KIT DAYS?

Keep In Touch or 'KIT' days are a useful way for you to stay in touch with work while you are on maternity leave. They allow you to do up to 10 days' work during your maternity leave without bringing your maternity leave to an end or losing Statutory Maternity Pay (SMP). KIT days can only take place if you and your employer want them to – you cannot be made to work during your maternity leave and you cannot demand to work. You cannot work during compulsory maternity leave, which is the two weeks following the birth of your child. There is nothing in the current UK legislation about how much an employee should be paid, although it is common practice for employers to top up your maternity leave to your usual level of pay for each day worked.

KIT days are particularly useful for team events or training opportunities, although they can be used for any form of work. Your employer may even run company-wide KIT days which are designed to welcome you and other mothers back into the organization.

> 'Part of our "best practice" is to get managers to discuss what contact the maternity leaver wants with her team while she is off, e.g. minutes of team meetings, monthly newsletters, etc. I

think that this is essential for feeling part of the organization while off work.

'Again, as part of a caring organization we are used to people bringing in their babies to show off to their colleagues. However, there gets to a point when the mum has "hung around" the office for too long and brings considerable disruption to business continuity. Therefore it's always advisable to pop in around lunchtime.'

When Julie, a management accountant, was on her second maternity leave, her company sent her business update emails and she had informal contact with her colleagues as well as going along to team away days. She says that having those links and knowing what was going on – without being under pressure to respond to emails – made her feel more confident about going back.

Kimberley also enjoyed formal KIT days at the school where she teaches, and advises women to be proactive about organizing them:

In terms of easing the transition I did go into work for meetings both times after my children were born, which was a nice taster of the world of work (made me check I could fit into my suit, etc.). My KIT days were fantastically easy to organize – I just told our bursar that I was coming in for a meeting and could it be a KIT day and she said yes. I would say, though, that you have to be proactive, find out through a friend still working there/supportive boss which are good days to come in and then ask for them. I think they won't ask you otherwise – it really needs to be initiated by you or bosses will feel that they are imposing.

Sarah, a solicitor in a financial services company, says she didn't organize formal KIT days but found that something as simple as keeping an eye on her emails made her feel connected:

> I kept my work email so that I kept abreast of what was happening. I was in fairly regular contact with work even if just to comment on an occasional email, and I also made myself available to deal with urgent queries from work. This meant that I didn't feel completely out of the loop when I returned.

> 'Always keep your employer informed of your plans, whether it be when you plan to return or likely changes to the hours you can work. Employers will be more flexible (well, most will be!) if you are open with them.'

If, on the other hand, you left the building, closed the door tightly and waddled away as fast as your bladder would let you, you might be feeling a little apprehensive about getting in touch and making your return. As an employee you are only legally required to do the following things to keep in touch:

- Tell your employer of your child's birth if he comes before your maternity leave starts or if you return within six months of his birth

- If you plan to return to work before the end of your statutory entitlement of 52 weeks, you need to put it in writing at least eight weeks beforehand.

> 'I think KIT days are brilliant – but not many people know about them. For both my maternity leaves I was offered the opportunity to come in and keep in touch while I was off. However, getting

childcare was really difficult for me, so I had to turn these days down. Although, yes, you get paid for them – it's not about the money: it's difficult leaving your young child with people who don't really know her (or people that you don't really trust).

Whether your first contact to discuss your return is a phone call, email or in-person visit will depend on whom it is you plan to speak to and your relationship with them. A short email may be the most comfortable thing to do. This is my 'second-time-comeback' email to The Mind Gym, a coaching organization I do freelance work for:

From: Jessica Chivers [mailto:jessica@beyoubutbetter.co.uk]
Sent: 20 January 2009 12:18
To: Richard Graham; Laura Turk
Subject: Getting Going Again!

Hi Laura and Graham,

Hope you are both brimming with goodness and enjoying some interesting projects at the moment. I am well and bubbling with enthusiasm for getting back into coaching. Not that it ever actually stopped! I've been asked to do a talk at The Vitality Show in March which is very exciting and I just gave you a call to have a chat about how I can get involved with goings-on at The Mind Gym. (I think a message has been left – not sure who the nice lady was that I spoke to.) I realize I probably need to speak to Karen but as we haven't met I thought I'd start by saying a quick hello to you both.

Anyway, I'm thinking ahead and getting organized. I'm hoping to start doing some workouts in April and would love to talk and get an update on how the business has progressed since I last delivered (in August). Hope you can fill me in at some point.

Pictures attached of my lovely lad and lass on Christmas day – time really is flying.

J.

Best wishes,

Jessica Chivers

It's worth seeing your return to work as a new start and viewing yourself as having licence to be as positive, proactive and assertive as you can – even if you weren't particularly any of those things before you went away. The more solution-focused you are, the better the response you are likely to get. We don't need research to tell us that good feelings rub off on others (but they do), and indeed they did when I got this equally upbeat response from head of the coaching network, Richard Graham. After having Artemis I was doing my first coaching assignment six months after she was born and it felt great:

> **From:** Richard Graham [mailto:Richard.Graham@ themindgym.com]
> **Sent:** 20 January 2009 14:20
> **To:** Jessica Chivers, Karen Sargent
> **Subject:** RE: Getting Going Again!
>
> Hi Jess
>
> How great to hear from you. I can't speak for Laura but I have certainly hit the New Year with lots of energy which is good considering how busy we are. It sounds like you have managed to keep your hand in with work and your profile high during your supposed time off. I'll look forward to finding out more.
>
> I've copied Karen in so that she can arrange to give you a call and meet up to chat about how we can get you up and running with some more workouts and of course meet our new team member!
>
> Take care
>
> Richard
>
> P.S. Great picture!

Thinking about your own approach to reconnecting with work, here are some ideas of what to say (or not).

DO SAY (even if it's not quite how you feel at this moment in time)	AVOID (because it's not the language of a confident comeback)
I'm looking forward to coming back and I've got a few ideas to run past you.	I can't wait to get away from all those stinky nappies and clearing food up off the floor – work will seem like a break.
Can we organize a mini-induction to bring me up to speed and help me settle back in, please?	I'm really nervous about coming back and feel like I won't have a clue about what's going on.
When's the next team meeting before I'm due back? I'd like to come in and say hello and get a feel for what's happening at the moment.	When do you want me?
My preference is to come back on or around the 10th November – how does that fit with you and the rest of the team?	My SMP runs out on the 9th November so shall I come back on the 10th?
When are you free in the next two weeks for us to get together for a chat and a catch-up on me coming back? The best dates for me are XXX – are any of these good for you?	I'll wait to hear from you about when I should come in for a meeting.
As we chatted about briefly before I went on maternity leave, I've thought through how I could work flexibly in a way that would suit the team and fit with the childcare I've organized. Only a few small changes in mind – be good to discuss this when we meet.	I've only got childcare Monday to Thursday and I'll need to leave at 4 p.m. on Mondays and Tuesdays so I can't do X on Monday afternoons and I won't be able to do Y on a Friday any more. Apart from that I'm easy.

RENEGOTIATING YOUR ROLE

In the previous chapter we started thinking about your preferences for returning to your 'old' role versus a move to a new organization. Let's nudge that black-and-white thinking into grey territory and consider a revamped version of your 'old' job.

> *'If you want to alter your hours, show how this could benefit your employer.'*

Things are bound to have moved on at least a little while you have been away, and with your fresh pair of eyes you may be able to suggest a reworking of your role and responsibilities to fit with what else is going on in your team and the wider organization. If your organization is particularly keen to get you back, now is a good time to negotiate changes you would like to make. As one mother whose skills are in demand told me,

It's important to negotiate hard when you agree to go back, to get what you want such as hours, days, the nature of your work, flexibility. You may not get another chance to specify these things, and if they are desperate to get you back they may just agree.

> 'Some things I wish I had done when I returned to work between my first and second children:
>
> 1. got a new job description
>
> 2. asked to work one day a week from home (I found when I did work from home I was far more productive than in the office)
>
> 3. clarified my key tasks and discussed which was a priority

> *4. held my hand up and said when my workload got too much.*
> *The reason I didn't was because I was worried it would be*
> *a 'mark' against me and they would be less likely to offer me*
> *flexible working in the future.'*

A good friend of mine who works as a solicitor for a County Council did just that. She looked at the key responsibilities and activities of each of the solicitors on her team and spotted an opportunity to reduce the workload of the solicitors within her team (by taking away a specific obligation) and taking responsibility for that aspect of their role herself. The tasks in question are things most of her team don't enjoy (and she does) and this means that the team benefits and my friend does work she enjoys in her preferred hours. It was a win-win situation, happy team, happy employee.

> *'Before going on maternity leave I held a generalist HR role,*
> *supporting the company's UK R&D business. I asked to return to*
> *work four days a week and was told that I could only do so if I*
> *adopted a different role. This was probably the right decision as*
> *it was a big job and I worked long hours, but a part of me was*
> *disappointed that I couldn't have it all. However, deep down I*
> *knew that I wouldn't have been able to pull it off – I'm not Wonder*
> *Woman! – and my family life would have suffered. In my new role*
> *I'm working on longer-term background HR projects. It's a big*
> *adjustment to make and I miss the frontline action of working*
> *with the business every day, but overall I'm really enjoying being*
> *back at work. I don't think my daughter would get the best of me*
> *if I were a full-time mother.'*

Legally speaking, if you return to work after Ordinary Maternity Leave (OML) you have the right to return to the job you were doing before you left. If you return after this, you usually still have the right to return to the same job, although under unusual circumstances you may be offered a similar role with the same terms and conditions. OML describes the first 26 weeks of your maternity leave, while Additional Maternity Leave (AML) refers to the second 26 weeks. All employees, regardless of the length of service or hours worked, are entitled to 52 weeks' maternity leave.

EXERCISE:

Do You Need to Renegotiate Your Role?

Get your notebook or a piece of paper and divide a page into three columns headed, 'Pros', 'Cons' and 'Ideal Solution.'

Thinking about your 'old' job (the one you left before having children and are considering returning to), jot down what comes to mind when you read these questions:

1. **What are the potential or actual plus points for going back to it? (PROS)**

2. **What are the potential or actual drawbacks of it? (CONS)**

3. **What would you need to change to mitigate the drawbacks and make your old job a suitable role for you now? (IDEAL SOLUTION)**

Having your thoughts in black and white can make it easier to see what's good about what you already have and/or spur you on to see what changes you need to make. If you've got a few things in the 'Ideal Solution' box think about how you can position your requests in a way that makes your team want to accommodate you – that is, what's in it for them?

If the balance looks tipped in the 'Cons' favour and you can't see a way to renegotiate your existing role, think about the questions again from the perspective of making a fresh start, in a new job (in a new organization).

THE 'F' WORD (FLEXIBILITY)

In my work I've noticed the least stressed mothers tend to be the most flexible and open ones. (I'm talking about minds not pelvises here!) While you might not always have demonstrated it before you had a child, I'm sure you've noticed how much more flexible and adaptable you have become. Just take for example the way you handle an average day with young children. You start with one plan (sorry, rough sketch – most of us quickly learn that having a 'plan' usually leads to disappointment and frustration) for the day and then mould and reshape it to fit around unexpected incidents, tantrums, accidents, whims and goodness knows what else. A loosely planned day can morph out of all recognition yet still be a success because we are such masters of flexibility. I'd put £50 on empirical research demonstrating mothers to be the most successful project managers for this reason. We are great at dealing with unforeseen events decisively and positively whilst minimizing disruption and discomfort to all concerned.

'In my experience it is vital to have a flexible employer even if they do not have official flexible working. As I'd always had flexible employers, I'd made an assumption that my new company wouldn't mind me leaving a few minutes early and making up the time during the day (at least twice over!). I was wrong. My employer was very inflexible about start and leave times, insisting that staff stayed until a set time, which meant I had to change my children's nursery as I would have been late picking up the children every day.'

Greater Flexibility Means Greater Satisfaction

My own conjecture aside, there *is* research to show that employees who are able to work flexibly (i.e. adjust their work hours as needed) report improved work–family balance and greater job satisfaction (Hill, 2001). This has to be good for employers as well as employees. Mental health scientists are sufficiently convinced of the benefits of flexible working to our well-being: in 2009 the National Institute for Health and Clinical Excellence (NICE) recommended flexible working where possible in its 'Promoting mental well-being at work' guidance.

> *'Be very flexible and seize opportunities – or make them!'*

It's rare to see a job ad these days that doesn't ask for 'highly-motivated, *flexible*, self-starters' or words to that effect. Yet how many employers demonstrate a genuinely flexible attitude in return? Some do and do it well, many don't. Let's face it, flexibility has to be a two-way street for it to work. According to a survey of 3,000 people for the Department for Work and Pensions, 50 per cent of people do not know which employees have a right to request flexible working, so you might need to make your employer aware (see the fact boxes below on flexible working legislation).

Progressive organizations may have flexible working policies which incorporate and even go beyond current UK legislation, but in practice it comes down to the person and the team you work with being willing to be flexible. It's people, not policies that make the decisions, and working parents' experiences of flexible working can vary inside the same organization.

What Flexibility Means to You

For many mothers, employer flexibility is crucial to a successful return to work. Your employers' attitude towards the 'f' word may well be the deciding factor in whether you climb aboard or jump ship. Flexibility might mean the following things:

- working from home when your child is ill

- compressed hours

- school hours only

- part-time hours

- coming in early, leaving early

- coming in late, leaving late

- a specifically timed lunch break to nip out to see your child(ren)

- guaranteed time off in school holidays

- making up lost days/hours due to a child's illness rather than having to use holiday entitlement

- working from home

- different hours during term-time and school holidays

'I think employers get a FANTASTIC deal out of working mothers. We're focused, can multi-task, usually really want to be at work and enjoy it. Try extra hard to justify a part-time role or a job-share because of this.'

Flexibility can mean a lot of different things and it is important to work out what sort of flexibility you need in order to be able to return to work. What does flexibility mean to you? What would you like versus what do you need? You might find it useful to write down your thoughts on those questions to clarify your thinking.

There are many reasons why organizations should want to adopt flexible working practices. For example, in *Changing Times*, the Trades Union Congress (TUC) reported in 2009 that over half the workforce believe they suffer ill-health resulting from a work–life imbalance. In contrast, workers with greater job flexibility report higher job satisfaction, and 8 in 10 employers believe this flexibility has a positive effect on job retention.

In an ideal world, flexible working would be easy, positive and smooth for both you and your employer. Each of us would work with a cooperative mindset, actively looking for opportunities to help colleagues work as efficiently and effectively as possible so we could all achieve a decent balance between work and others aspects of our lives. Those of us who request flexible ways of working would be equally prepared to accommodate our employers' requests as much as possible, too. But, achieving the ideal is not usually the story in the majority of workplaces, so let's consider how to achieve the best possible outcomes.

7 Steps to Achieving a Suitable Flexible Working Arrangement

1. **Find out about your organization's flexible working policy.** Your organization may have a flexible working policy, but how it is translated and applied can vary, particularly in large organizations where roles and attitudes can differ significantly. Happily for some women – and sadly for others – flexible working seems to be heavily influenced by the

style of the 'flexee's' boss. Bosses or line managers with a more trusting and relaxed management style may be more likely to support flexible working than bosses who like to micromanage.

2. **Keep an open mind about what it is possible to achieve.** You may have heard positive or negative stories from other employees about flexible working requests, but don't make assumptions about what this means for you. See your request as a separate, fresh case to be judged on its own merits and you might be pleasantly surprised.

3. **Consider the situation from the perspective of your boss and the rest of the team.** People are persuaded to do something for their own reasons, not ours, which means it usually pays to consider the world from the perspectives of the interested parties when building a case for flexible working. What's in it for them? How will your proposed way of working be of benefit to more than just you? What would make you say 'yes' if the boot were on the other foot? Think about the drawbacks to your proposals, too, and acknowledge them in your conversation.

4. **Separate what you *need* from what you would *like*.** You are likely to have some flexibility requirements that will make or break a job deal. For instance, it might be absolutely crucial that you are able to leave at 4.30 every day and if the job won't allow that then you may have to rethink the role (or your childcare arrangements). On the other hand, only working term-time or working from home one day a week might be nice, but not a necessity. Drawing up a list of what you need versus what is a nice-to-have can help you clarify your situation in your own mind as well as preparing you to have a confident conversation with your boss.

5. **Create a solution to a problem.** Whoever said 'You're either part of the problem or part of the solution' was onto

something. Which one are you? You may be able to pitch your flexible working request as a solution to a 'problem' that is either obvious or hasn't been spotted by the powers that be. Like Lou at the beginning of this chapter, you might suggest only working term-time (if that's what you need) would be of greater benefit to the organization than working year-round. Positioning your preferred way of working as a solution – rather than a problem for someone else to solve – might require more than a moment's thought but will be well worth it if it means you get what you would like.

'When I returned from maternity leave, I negotiated four days a week. In that role, it was acceptable. Then two months later I was promoted, and was expected to do five days a week. I managed to negotiate one day 'working from home', which worked for a short while but then I increased my childcare to four-and-a-half days a week. About six months later I called it quits in that job (glass ceiling syndrome) but it took another four months to get out. I then went down to three days a week. I was in a strong bargaining position, as nobody wanted to lose me. I chose my role and my days. I worked this pattern for another year and felt it worked and then went on my second maternity leave. I returned to three days a week and, if I had remained in paid employment, I probably would have continued but I wanted more flexibility in my life and a more interesting career, so went self-employed.'

6. **Seek support, find allies.** Who in your team or wider organization has the ear of your boss? Who can play a hand in getting the go-ahead for your flexible working request? For instance, if you suss out your colleagues first and they are warm to your plans, you could use this to help persuade your boss. Or perhaps there is a good story of another colleague working flexibly which you can use to demonstrate how it would work. Be aware of (not) positioning your re-

quest as a kind of 'Well she's doing it, so why can't I?' type thing as that does nothing for your reputation and it undermines the trusting, mature work environment you have (or hope to achieve) in your organization.

7. **Discuss your proposal, be prepared to negotiate.** 'Flexible' is the operative word when it comes to having flexible working discussions. The clear picture you have in mind about your ideal scenario may not translate into the same beautiful scene in your boss' mind so you might need to flex your ideas in the light of his or her perspective. Maintaining a positive mindset and believing you can come to a mutually agreeable arrangement will help to make it happen. Try and see your negotiations as a collaborative conversation where you both come out feeling good. Collaboration is about finding a win-win which might look, feel or sound different to how you originally imagined. Keeping an open mind is key.

FLEXIBLE WORKING LEGISLATION – ELIGIBILITY

In a Nutshell

As a parent with a child under 17 (18 if he or she has a disability) you have the right to *apply* for flexible working, not the right to have it.

The Detailed Version

As of April 6th 2009, an eligible employee who is (or is the spouse, civil partner or live-in partner of) the parent, adoptive parent, guardian, special guardian or foster parent of a child under the age of 17 (or of a child with a disability under the age of 18), and who has a need to spend more time with that child, has the legal right to apply to his or her employer for a more flexible pattern of working hours or (where appropriate) the opportunity to work from home.

An individual applying for a more flexible pattern of working hours must be an 'employee' in the strict legal sense of the word, i.e. he or she must be employed under a contract of service. You must:

- have been continuously employed by your employer for at least 26 weeks at the time the application is made;

- submit your application by the day before the child's 17th birthday (or the child's 18th birthday, if he or she has a disability);

- have, or expect to have, responsibility for the child

- not have submitted an earlier application to work flexibly within the previous 12 months, regardless of whether the previous application was made in relation to the same caring responsibility or a different one.

Some mothers say they feel there is so much riding on their application for flexible working that they feel nervous about having the conversation. You might want to drop an email to your boss outlining your ideas *before* you have a chat about it, or rehearse the conversation with a friend or partner before you do it for real.

FLEXIBLE WORKING LEGISLATION – APPLICATIONS & APPROVAL

An application for flexible working must be made in writing and must:

- state that it is an application for a change to the terms and conditions of employment

- specify the change applied for and the date on which it is proposed the change will become effective

- explain what effect (if any) you think making the change applied for would have on your employer and how, in your opinion, any effect might be dealt with

- explain the employee's relationship to the child or adult in question

- state whether a previous application for flexible working has been made by the employee to the employer and, if so, when

- be dated.

Within 28 days of receiving an eligible employee's application for flexible working, your employer must either accept the application and notify you in writing, or arrange a meeting with you to discuss the application. Within 14 days of the meeting, the employer must write to you either:

- agreeing to the application and specifying the contract variation agreed and the start date on which it is to take effect; or

- refusing the application and stating which of the specified grounds for refusal it considers to be applicable and
  explaining why those grounds apply in relation to the application.

An employer's refusal to accept an eligible employee's
application for flexible working must be based on one
or more specific grounds. These are:

- the burden of additional costs;

- a detrimental effect on ability to meet customer demand;

- an inability to reorganize work among existing staff or re-
  cruit additional staff;

- a detrimental impact on quality or performance;

- insufficiency of work during the periods the employee
  proposes to work;

- planned structural changes; or

- such other grounds as may be specified in regulations
  made by the Secretary of State.

SHAPING EXPECTATIONS, SETTING BOUNDARIES

Working Hours

As for the teacher who told us her story about asking for
part-time work (page 60), perhaps taking work home with
you is entirely appropriate, especially if it is part of your pre-

ferred way of working and/or you are rewarded for it. For other women, taking work home is not something they want to do. How would it be if you could contain your workload within your agreed hours? Or if you could leave work on time every day without anybody batting an eyelid? How about nobody hassling you on 'non-working' days? It's definitely possible to achieve these things – or variations personal to you – and setting expectations and sticking to boundaries is how you can make it happen.

> 'With my work before I had children, if there was a busy period I would have stayed late to get things finished, but now I didn't have that option and had to work within strict hours. I occasionally did work from home, but found that I would only have about an hour in the evening and the last thing I wanted to do was to continue working.'

Before you had children you may have been quite flexible about how much time you spent at work. Maybe it was easy to accommodate peaks and troughs in your team's workload, and perhaps you didn't think twice about staying late to meet deadlines, coming in early or working away from home. Now you have children you probably cannot or do not want to offer the same level of flexibility. Or maybe you would like to and it is a source of frustration for you that your childcare doesn't accommodate it.

Explain Your Situation to Colleagues

While children, childminders, penalty fees for late nursery pick-ups and 'absolutely-must-make-the-16.39 train' type thoughts have been swimming round your head for goodness knows how long, your boss and your colleagues may be clueless about the importance of these things in your life. Your team might not necessarily appreciate how much things have changed in your world outside work – especially if they don't have children – so you need to let them know enough about how things are different for you to be able to work well together.

> 'What I have been disappointed by is the way some people judge me now, just because I'm a mum. I can see that they have already consigned me to a bench on the side, whereas I was considered to be a "rising star" before and was in on all the action. I can tell that now some people dismiss my potential contribution because they're just waiting for me to go off on maternity leave again. They also think I'm less committed because I work part-time, when actually I'm achieving more in less time.'

For your sake, as well as theirs, you need to explain how you are adapting the way you work to accommodate your other priorities. It doesn't mean you are not as committed or cannot make adjustments to your work schedule (so long as you are given enough notice). It just means flexibility isn't to be expected at the drop of a hat. Remember, if your colleagues are to respect your boundaries, you need to respect them, too.

If the way you hope to manage your work commitments now is different from the way you operated before, it helps to be as clear and confident about this from the moment you return. Shaping your bosses' and colleagues' expectations is the key to good relationships with them, and by being upfront and clear about needing to leave at 4.30 on the dot every day, for instance, you needn't feel embarrassed or awkward. So many women I know say they hate getting up to leave before everyone else and looking like a 'shirker', but if you explain your way of working and demonstrate your commitment to the team, they are more likely to understand.

Before I had children I worked with a woman called Jackie who, in my opinion at least, managed full-time work with two children beautifully. She was a valued member of the team and a great role model on many levels. If something came up that needed dealing with as she was about to dash off, she would ask one of the team if they could give her a call on her mobile when she was on the train so they could discuss it and sort it out between them. Her being out of the office and on her way home just wasn't an issue because she was flexible in her attitude about taking calls and helping out once she had left for the day.

'Du Temps Pour Vivre'

It is the nature of the way we work in the UK that there will always be more to do than we can get done during the hours we are contracted to do, and if you enjoy your work you may have ideas and tasks you feel you cannot or do not want to leave until the next time you are in. However, if you have decided to work part-time you clearly *want* to give equal priority to something other than your professional life, and you need to remember that. The French have a name for it: *Du temps pour vivre,* which means 'more time for everyday life'.

> 'Don't arrange to work at home while looking after your children
> – you will never get anything done.'

On your non-working days your number-one priority is probably time with your children and your partner, followed by time with your friends and time for you to relax and pursue other interests (more on this in the Mantra 8 chapter). A study of working parents in four European countries, led by Dr Margret Fine-Davis, found that more than 75 per cent of mothers and fathers wanted more or much more time for themselves, and about the same numbers wanted to spend more or much more time with their families. The desire is there and we have to make it happen by drawing boundaries and working to them.

In the words of a passionate and committed HR professional:

As a part-time worker I'm strict about my days off – I'm no longer paid to work on those days so why should I be available? You need to start as you mean to go on and set clear expectations about your (non) availability outside your normal work week. Otherwise people won't respect your work days and you'll suffer from work creepage. This will have an impact on your home life and, although you think you're helping, you'll probably be perceived as not being fully dedicated to the job (as people making the demands on you can easily forget that you're actually not supposed to be available on that day/time). I see time at home with my family as sacrosanct and will not compromise it by routinely taking work home with me. It's unlikely you'll be rewarded for it at work. There may be exceptional occasions where it is really necessary and I'd be willing to 'go the extra mile' for my job, but your family needs your attention at home and if you do have any time left over you should use that to recharge your batteries, so that you can sustain your levels of activity and be an even better employee and mother.

> 'I have to remind myself at times that I am working to live, not living to work, and therefore to step back and not keep doing overtime.'

What are your thoughts on where your boundary lies when it comes to work on non-working days? Is it acceptable? Do you feel it is impossible not to work on non-working days? Take yourself through the Your Work–Home Boundaries exercise below to develop your personal policy on how you would like to manage your professional life.

Exercise
Your Work–Home Boundaries

To think about your work–home boundaries is to start to bring them to life. Close your eyes and imagine how you would ideally organize your workload so that it stays within the boundaries you set. Be bold, be brave – really think about what you would like right down to the smallest detail. For example, what time do you want to be back at home? Will you take phone calls on your non-working days? If yes, is there a time limit or a certain time you would like people to call? Are you happy to work beyond your official hours to get the job done? If yes, how will you realistically do this given your childcare arrangements? When you leave work, is that it for the day? Or does checking your emails in the evening fall within your boundaries?

Write down what your boundaries are on the following things:

- email

- using your Blackberry/iPhone for work-related issues out-side office hours

- phone calls when you are not in the office

- working before you arrive at work

- working after you have left the office

- working while you are travelling into/out of work

- lunchtimes

- non-working days

- weekends

- evenings

- coming into work on non-working days

- taking part in meetings or conference calls outside your hours.

You can revisit your notes every so often to remind yourself what plans and promises you've made.

EASING YOURSELF IN GENTLY

For the last however many months or years, your days have probably been non-stop, go-go-go, busy-busy-busy meeting the needs of your young family. And of course you know that's not about to change! But your return to work as an event in itself needn't be that gung-ho. In fact, if you've got the opportunity to do it, you probably want to ease yourself in gently. Women who make a smooth return say they allowed themselves time to get into their stride and build their confidence; a bit like we do with our kids when we introduce them to a new nursery, childminder or school.

Project worker Lee-Rose describes her return:

The first few weeks of work were quite relaxing and I was easing myself into things gradually. But after those few weeks it was like I was hit by a whirlwind. I started working on two new projects at the same time and there was a lot to do to get them started. A lot of the tasks I was doing were new to me and I had to do them in a very quick timescale. There was a period of two or three weeks when I felt very stressed. I didn't get a chance to get used to being back at work and also having two boys to look after. It has taken me a while to get used to it all and handling the stress, and the last month of work has been easier, but then a different difficult phase started when illnesses arose – the boys became ill and then I was ill a few times with different things, and this was difficult juggling everything and also trying to get my work done. I went into work ill a few times. I managed to get through that and now everything is running smoothly again. I think there will always be phases like this.

Use Your Holiday Allowance

Perhaps you have accrued holiday allowance that could allow you to work a three-day week, as opposed to four or five days, for the first month. Or you might be able to work a shorter day for the first fortnight. It might not be possible to work different hours for this short period – and you might not want to if you're the sort of person who prefers to get stuck in from the off – but it's worth considering. It could make all the difference to the way you settle back in and perform. It's up to you to ask, because your team doesn't necessarily know your preferences and they might not know how a staggered start could help you (and them).

> 'The week before I went back I got myself and the kids up, dressed and out of the house just as I would have to when I was back at work properly. It was weird being suited and booted but it got me feeling ready for it all. After dropping the children at nursery I stayed out of the house, caught up on some work stuff my boss had sent through in a coffee shop and met one of my colleagues for lunch. It was like an unofficial first day back and it meant I felt much calmer on my actual first day back. It sounds a bit sad but it worked for me!'

Remember, as part of Statutory Maternity Leave the Government allows maternity leavers to do up to ten paid days' work during maternity leave as a way of keeping in touch. These KIT days could be a way to ease you back in. See page 63.

When you picture yourself back at work, how do you imagine you'll feel? Nervous? Stressed? Excited? Energized? Are you relaxed and working at a comfortable pace or rushed, frantic and feeling there's never enough time? It's worth thinking about how you want to feel when you go back, so you can do your best to prepare to feel that way. If you set yourself up to start well there's a much better chance that you will make that way of working a habit. Try the exercise below (Easing Yourself Back into Work) to help you visualize how you want to approach your return to work.

Many mothers say that the settling-in period for their children at childminders, nurseries or with nannies has been crucial to their preparation for going back to work. Having this bit of time to yourself before you go back helps you to prepare mentally and get organized. It is a period of transition where you can start to think like a working woman again, perhaps by doing your journey to work, wearing 'work' clothes or doing something connected to your work to help get you back in the zone.

> *'Stagger your return, do not go straight in full-time. That way it is not so much of a shock to the system.'*

There is much more about preparing to go back and re-adjusting in the Mantra 7 chapter Prepare for a Smooth Return, and a section on settling your child into the care you have organized in the Mantra 4 chapter Find Childcare that Fits Your Family.

Exercise
Easing Yourself Back into Work

This is a nice one to do in the bath, maybe with a glass of wine or some relaxing candles to help you mellow.

Breathing calmly and deeply from your belly, close your eyes, allow your mind to unwind and conjure up images of you making a smooth and calm return to work. You are visualizing your ideal scenario and you need focus only on what you would like to happen, not how to make it happen.

Here are some questions to set your mind wandering:

- What contact will you have had with your colleagues before your official return?

- What are you doing the day before you go back to work?

- How are you relaxing and getting ready the night before?

- What is happening before you get to work on your first day?

- Who is getting your child(ren) ready and who is looking after them?

- How are you getting to work?

- What are you doing when you get to work?

- Whom are you meeting with for an update?

- How are you spending your lunch break?

- How are you making sure you get away on time at the end of the day?

- How are you spending the evening of your first day?

- How many days are you doing in your first week?

- How are you resting and enjoying yourselves as a family at the end of your first week?

You might find it useful to make a note of your answers when you're out of the bath (unless your partner will sit on the loo and scribe for you) so you can remind yourself of what you're trying to achieve and how you're going to do it.

KEY IDEAS & ACTION POINTS

The working mum's mantra for this chapter is 'Keep in touch and ask for what you want.'

- **Asking for what you want** is compatible with being nice. Be proactive about managing your return to work and asking for the way you would like to work. Keep in mind the mums we've heard from in this chapter, who achieved part-time or term-time work by making it look attractive to their employers.

- **Confidence:** You were good at your job before you had a child, and that hasn't changed. 'Con' isn't in the word 'confidence' for nothing – you might need to fake it 'til you make it in the first few weeks.

- **Keep in touch:** Mums says it's easier to go back if you've stayed in touch with colleagues. Talk to your boss about Keep In Touch (KIT) days or a staggered return to help you have a smooth transition back to work.

- **Flexible working:** It is important to consider your request for flexible working from your team's perspective as well as your own. Use the seven steps to arranging flexible working (page 76) to help you work out what you need versus what you would like and to prepare for the conversation with your boss.

- **Work–Home Boundaries:** Know what your boundaries are and help your team to understand how you might be working differently to the way you did before. Communication is key to good working relationships – how will you set expectations?

MUM'S MANTRA

3

See Your Family as a Team

The most important thing a father can do for his children is to love their mother.

THEODORE HESBURGH

You've thought about what you want at work and know how to ask for it; now let's take that and apply it at home with our working mum's mantra number three: *See your family as a team*.

Given that nearly 7 in 10 of the mothers I surveyed say their partners believe that their going back to work is best for the family, I reckon it's only right and reasonable that *the family* gets involved in helping make mum's return to work, work. Whether 'family' means you, partner and baby or you, estranged husband, two foster kids and a mother-in-law (like one of the mums I heard from) it's the attitude, not the make-up that counts.

> *'Being back at work makes you work together as a team even more than before. We share pick-up and drop-off and the cooking. When Alex is ill my husband is often the one to deal with it.'*

GETTING YOUR MINDSET RIGHT

Towards the end of my second maternity 'slowdown' (as in foot off the self-employment accelerator but not actually on the brake) I felt fat, knackered and in need of a wife. Not a husband, a wife. I felt overloaded, fed up and frazzled, and looking back part of this was probably because I hadn't got my team mindset right.

Incidentally, it's no wonder I wanted a wife when you consider that even when both father and mother work full-time, on average the woman still does more of every domestic duty than the man and men tend to over-report the amount they do (Fine-Davis *et al.*, 2004).

> *'I have a fully supportive husband who believes that the mother's happiness is key to the family's happiness as she is the central figure. He understood completely why I was not being fulfilled by being a full-time mum and supported my return to work.'*

Then I started to imagine I was the maître d' and co-owner of a swanky restaurant. I imagined that my business partners had asked me to work back of house three days a week and, fancying the challenge and wanting to fly the flag of teamwork, I'd agreed but only on the basis that I dished out some of my front-of-house responsibilities to others on the team (because, of course, trying to do both would probably send me bonkers and be bad for business). By thinking of my domestic responsibilities as if they were a business it became easier to see how it was up to me to say how best to share the load. Like the maître d', I believe when us mothers go back to work we need to renegotiate our role at home and think like a team to keep everyone and everything together.

The family-as-team mindset starts with us recognizing that there needs to be a shift in the way we view ourselves and our role within the family. Unless you believe you are Wonder Woman (capable of throwing a part- or full-time job into the domestic mix with no apparent side effects), you probably need to rethink how you'll blend domesticity with work. You're amazing, for sure, but Wonder Woman is a fiction created by a man. Unless you can ditch or delegate some of the responsibilities you've had at home whilst you've been away from work, you're going to be one fed-up, washed-out and resentful ex-superhero six months down the line.

Exercise

What Do You Expect from Yourself?

Let's take a moment to focus exclusively on your expectations of yourself – both the conscious and until now perhaps *unconscious* ones. Forget about other people; this is just about you. Do this when you've got a chance to think undisturbed, maybe when baby is down for a nap.

Divide a piece of paper into two columns, on the left put the heading MY BELIEFS and on the right put the heading NEW REALITY.

In the left-hand column write down what comes to mind when you reflect on these questions:

- What do I assume my life will be like as a working mother?

- What domestic/personal responsibilities do I think I need to continue doing when I am back at work?

- How much time do I anticipate I will have to devote to family life?

- What other expectations do I have about myself?

Looking at what you have written down in the left-hand column, are your expectations reasonable? What would you think if a friend said she expected these things of herself?

On the right-hand side of the page under the heading NEW REALITY write down how you could change the things you don't like about what you have written in the left-hand column. For instance, maybe you reflect that you probably won't have time to do all the housework yourself so you're not going to. Perhaps you see that you would like to have more family time, and to do that you need to do less of something else. Think about actions you can take to make your NEW REALITY happen and write them down. This is a self-reflection exercise and it doesn't need to be neat and tidy. Scrawling over the page is fine! The point is for you to see in black and white whether your expectations of yourself are either bang on the money or need tweaking (and what those newly tweaked expectations look like).

PARTNER UP

Some 92 per cent of the women I surveyed said they are completely honest with their partners about their reasons for returning to work. Does your partner know how you feel about returning to work? Does he understand what's driving your return?

> 'I think getting my husband to take the majority of the responsibility at the beginning then gradually taking it back helped his attitude. It's hard for them to adjust to helping out when you have been at home and they have not had to think about drop-offs, pick-ups and everything else.'

Samantha credits sharing her work motivations with her husband as an important part of them working as a team:

My husband knows and appreciates how much I value my work and how big a part of me it is. We both knew

I would go back to work after maternity leave and we devised a joint plan to enable that. He does the 'morning shift' with our daughter and I do the 'evening shift'. We also operate very much as a team, devising joint strategies on things like tantrums and night waking.

Mathilde's husband is open to ideas about how he and his wife combine work and home, and clearly recognizes her talents:

My wife is an extremely intelligent lady and I know she needs something else rather than just being Mummy, so I'm completely supportive of her going back to work. I could not spend all my time at home with the kids as it would drive me completely potty, so I fully respect the need to go and do something that stretches the old grey matter a bit more than playing with Lego. Who knows, we might both end up working part-time so that we can share looking after the kids and have some working life, too.

When we are explicit about our hopes and desires about work, family and how to combine the two, we're giving our partners the information they need to consider the part they could, should or need to play to make it happen. Sometimes it's simply by sharing and building the vision of what a happy family is, together – rather than talking about roles, responsibilities and how you'll divvy up domestic duties – that gets you the best outcome. I know we joke about men not being mind readers and needing to tell our men exactly what needs to be done, when and how, but the subtle suggestive route is probably a better starting point than bullishly

MOTHERS WORK!

telling him how things are going to be around here when you go back to work. Or even worse, not saying anything at all and soldiering on alone.

From my husband's mouth:

When Jessica gives me piecemeal jobs to do I switch off because it's dull, but if she makes a suggestion of what needs doing without directing me on how it should get done then I'll do it more willingly. I don't notice everything that she notices but I do have a domestic radar which I act on if I'm given the chance. We agree now that when I cook Jessica gets out of the kitchen and I do it my way – far better that she sees the end result and not the process because she slips into micromanaging me otherwise. It was a smart move her telling me about the psychology research that shows a correlation between men being more involved in housework and getting more sex (from their wives!).

'My husband wanted me to go back to work, although since being back we have considered the not-working option as there is no denying it is really, really hard sometimes. At times I rely too much on him and he has to remind me gently that I have to make this work and find compromises myself. We keep each other on track and when one of us takes on too much and cracks a little it swings back the other way. I know I am lucky that my husband is so good at doing his share, but I cannot see why he should not be doing so when we are both under the same pressures.'

Equality Isn't Dividing Things Down the Middle

My belief is that partnering up, like equality, is an attitude more than anything else. Equality is when you both recognize the need and see the merit in deciding together how you can best manage the totality of your lives. Equality doesn't mean you both having to do a bit of everything or contributing in the same way every day, as mum Hayley reflects:

My husband's job means that he is able to do very little on a regular or definite basis. I cannot rely on him to do a job all the time or assume that he has done it, for example deciding what we are having for dinner, or keeping on top of the washing. He's good at spotting what needs doing when he's at home and will do it without being asked – that's what matters.

'I think that Louisa and I share the needs of our daughter quite evenly between ourselves. There is no fixed pattern of roles; it really is down to looking at our diaries over the next few days and making things work. If I know I'm not going to be around, then Louisa makes sure she is, and vice versa. It makes for a bit of a hectic lifestyle, but we've never been that regimented in our schedule anyway.'

Jenny shares the same idea:

My husband works long hours and doesn't have the time, energy or inclination on a weekday evening to do anything around the house, so generally Monday to Friday everything household-related falls to me. On the one day I work from the office my husband does the morning drop-off so I can get to work early, enabling me to leave work early to pick the kids up. He is very good at the weekend, however, and is the bathroom-cleaning king.

Father of two Mike is often away from home with work and reflects that being a team is about noticing what needs doing and getting on with it when he's around:

Our domestic arrangements, just seemed to 'fall into place' from within days of our first child coming to our home from the maternity unit. We both would be doing child-related tasks in tandem, but without too much spoken instruction: one would be filling up the sterilizer while the other put on the hot water. Naturally we've had disagreements and the usual arguments and a few tears, but on the whole we work well together as a team. The company I work for have been very good at allowing me to work 'adjusted' hours, but this tends to mean more time on the Blackberry 'after hours'. The plus side is that I have, until recently, been able to work from home one day a week, which means I was able to do the school run. I also go into work late, enabling the whole family to have breakfast together.

> *'I feel hugely more resourceful, well and happy when my husband picks up the slack and thinks proactively about the needs of his young family. That's what teamwork is to me – sharing the thinking.'*

Sarah agrees that her definition of equality has developed since becoming a parent:

It's definitely taken me a while to work this out, as up until having children equality meant that in the true sense of the word, i.e. we both did the same things in equal portions, but since having Martha I think equality is really something different. I think it means discussing how you want to live your life as a family, appreciating what each other does and recognizing the important contributions you both make. That said, I think you'll always have moments of resentment, and for us that happens most when we don't communicate enough or when Martha is ill and we are both tired.

Aaahhhh yes, the 'T' word. Tiredness is that all-too-familiar blanket of fuzz that swaddles many a well-intentioned parent's brain and stops the teamwork attitude from shining through. It's on the-morning-after-the-disturbed-night-before, or the evening that follows an eventful day that you fully realize the benefits of having planned and scheduled the division of household labour (and blue-tacked it to the fridge so you both know exactly who's supposed to be doing what). If that sounds familiar and your family operates better with lists and charts, this probably works for you (and may have the added benefit of you both remembering just how much you both contribute). In this example, I've given our mum and dad the names Kim and Paul. Kim works three days a week (M/T/W). They have a weekly cleaner (C):

Category	DESCRIPTION	M	T	W	T	F	S	S	As needed
CHILDREN	Dress/breakfast/teeth clean	P	P	K	K	K	Both	Both	
CHILDREN	Nursery/childminder drop-off	P	P	K					
CHILDREN	Nursery/childminder pick-up	K	K	P					
CHILDREN	Make/organize dinner	K	K	P	K	K	Both	Both	
CHILDREN	Bathtime/Bedtime routine	K	P	P	P	P	Both	Both	
CHILDREN	Sterilize bottles/get stuff ready for tomorrow	K	K	P	K	K	P	P	
DOMESTIC	Plan meals for week								Kim
DOMESTIC	Do online shopping				K				
DOMESTIC	Put away online shopping delivery						P		
DOMESTIC	Top-up shopping								K/P
DOMESTIC	Make dinner	K	K	P	K	K	P	P	
DOMESTIC	Change beds					C			
DOMESTIC	Stay on top of laundry basket								Kim
DOMESTIC	Ironing								Paul
DOMESTIC	Quick clean of kitchen/stack dishwasher	K	K	P	K	K	P	P	
DOMESTIC	Full dust/clean of house					C			
FAMILY ORGANIZATION	Keep on top of nursery paperwork								Paul
FAMILY ORGANIZATION	Pay bills/keep eye on joint account								Paul
FAMILY ORGANIZATION	Organize car insurance, MOT, etc.								Kim
FAMILY ORGANIZATION	Remember birthdays								Kim
FAMILY ORGANIZATION	Night out – choir/running club	P			K				

A blank copy of this planner is available for free – you can download it from www.jessicachivers.com.

A Word on Resentment

Since Sarah mentioned resentment I'm game for sharing what I do about mine. I don't think I'd had any intra-marital resentment until we had children, but now I sometimes *resent* the apparent simplicity of my husband's life. I sometimes *resent* that his life is a stream of serially processed tasks, not a jumble of juggling as is mine. I sometimes *resen*t that he works full-time and I do not. In my most ungenerous hour (which used to be 3–4 p.m. on a wet winter afternoon as my patience withered with the setting sun, when our children were behaving no more or less than how a one-year-old and three-year-old behave and it was still four hours 'til bedtime), I think my husband's got it easy. From my perspective this is his life: get up, shower in peace whilst children sleep and wife makes packed lunch, drive to work listening to interesting podcast, do interesting problem-solving work, eat tasty lunch, do more interesting problem-solving and undisturbed thinking, drive back home and lose self in another stimulating podcast, be welcomed home by family eager to see him, eat second scrumptious home-made meal, spend hour being adored by children, enjoy restful evening. Repeat. Do you know what I mean?

> *'I was lucky in that my husband supported me totally in my decision to set up my business, although there are times when we have a bit of a niggle as I believe he feels his job is more important than mine – but as the main breadwinner he's probably right!'*

Then I get a grip of the Lego bricks and tell myself to stop rehearsing my thoughts into a sob story to spill when he comes home because actually I know his life is more complex than that. I tell myself we are a team and I have so much to be grateful for! I remember what I say to people I'm coaching about the power of empathizing with the person we want to win over, and as if by magic I notice aspects of his day that I don't envy at all. I see the totality of our lives and not just the odd crap afternoon; I begin to focus on what's good about our set-up, appreciate what he does for Team Chivers and hear his admiration for me ringing in my ears. All of which stops me from opening my mouth.

And then there are other times (like when I read research on the 'double-burden' of working mothers which describes how, by and large, women retain the same level of domestic and family responsibility when they return to work as they did when they were at home full-time) when I tell him I think he's got it easy. But only when we've both had enough sleep.

> 'My partner is exceptional in that he is always understanding when I have to work and takes on as much housework and looking after my daughter (not his) as he can. He understands my love of what I do, he asks me how initiatives are panning out and talks to me about what I'm doing. This is the opposite of my ex, who had decided that I was to be a stay-at-home mum with my business prioritized below the housework. He did not understand my need to work or my passion for my business, and would even get annoyed if I asked him to pick up food from the supermarket on the way home from work.'

Winning Over a Reluctant Partner

From resentment to reluctance, how do you handle a partner who's not keen on you going back to work, or doesn't buy into the family-as-team approach? Whilst 38 per cent of the women I surveyed said they felt pressure from their partner to return to work, 11 per cent said they thought their partners would rather they didn't.

If that's your situation, do you know his reasoning? Can you see where he's coming from? If you stand in his shoes and imagine the way he's interpreting your return to work, can you see what he finds unappealing about it? If it helps you to think, try writing down his possible objections and any solutions that might be useful.

My experience is that if we play up the positives of a situation – whilst acknowledging the downsides and how we can mitigate them – most people will be persuaded. The trick is to offer positives that appeal to the person we want to influence, and that's because people are persuaded for their reasons, not ours. Lawyer-turned-coach Catrin says:

I know that I am a better person all round if I am working. I know that I have important skills to share, and not being able to do that makes me frustrated. The fulfilment that work brings can have a positive effect on a woman's personality, which in turn has a knock-on effect on the family. When women are successful at work they are often more confident, energetic and have more of a zest for life, irrespective of what they earn. That energy is a great thing for a marriage.

> 'My husband makes a point of getting home most days in time to bath the children, and we take turns at reading at bedtime. He gets up in the night if the children wake because he copes better on less sleep than I do.'

Similarly, one of the mums I've spoken with paints a compelling picture of why supporting a woman if she wants to return to work is a good idea. She could be the voice of the majority of women I've spoken to:

> Going back to work has made me feel stronger and more energetic, and this enables me to be enthusiastic about life generally. Before I went back to work I felt like each day was the same, and even on holiday we would tend to go to self-catering cottages where I would continue to cook, tidy up, shop, etc. Now I feel like I have variety and more purpose in my life, and having work allows me to be a better wife, mother, daughter, sister, friend. I have more to talk about, I feel confident, I am enthusiastic and lively. Before work I felt like I cleaned, tidied, cooked, disciplined the children. Now I feel like I enjoy my time with my husband more. I feel more equal, I suppose.

> *'My husband is brilliant at the practical things. He does tons in the morning when I'm not fully functional, and when he washes my dry-clean-onlys I just think to myself it's better than having no help at all.'*

FAMILY AND FRIENDS ARE YOUR BIGGER TEAM

And what if you don't have a partner? Cue thinking about your wider support network of friends and family. Parents? Best mate? Neighbour? Parent-in-laws? Aunt? Brother? Paid help? If you're a self-reliant sort of woman you might not notice the amount of potential support that could be there for you; if you're proud or worried about what others might think, perhaps you stop short of asking. Putting aside those limiters, take a minute to consider and write down who is or could be there for you.

> 'My grandkids were the trigger for things changing in my life even though my daughter never asked me for help – I think because she didn't want to burden me. Moving closer to my grandchildren has given me something positive to focus on and that has helped me a great deal. I look after each of the grandchildren a day a week and it's good for me, helps my daughter a bit and saves money on childcare that she can put to other things. I think it's good for all of us.'

Writing for *The Times* Online's Alpha Mummy blog, in a prelude to an article about the charity Home-Start, columnist Jennifer Howze encourages us to ask for help when we need it:

One of the most maddening things about being middle-class is that no matter what your problems, you're just expected to get on with it. Depression, illness, family stress, the inability to cope when things go wrong – never mind those. We expect ourselves to buck up under the pressure and sort ourselves out because we have a decent home, steady jobs and vices that run merely to an extra glass of Pinot on the weekend. We don't need help, we tell ourselves, and wider society has much the same view. Government and organizations dealing with family problems focus their energies on poor families without resources, quite rightly. Yet we have to admit sometimes that we can't do it all on our own, no matter how well-adjusted, organized and proud we are.

'My parents live nearby and both are a great help. My mother (age 70) is very hands-on and will have them for a full day while I go on a course or a photo shoot – but she works part-time so this has to fit in around her working hours. My father is good at amusing them if I need to get work finished, and both help to pick them up from school/nursery when I ask them.'

Family members can be a huge emotional support wherever they are in the world. Jenny laments her mum:

I have no practical support on a day-to-day basis from extended family as they all live a million miles away, but my mother is amazing at propping up my self-esteem and reminding me that sometimes being a working mum ain't easy. I would say that on an average week I speak to my mum more than once a day, and that half of the conversations include some type of emotional support when I'm feeling that it's all too much.

Hayley feels that emotional support is one of the most valuable things her family does for her:

My husband, mother, father and sister are all good at listening to different aspects of my life. My mum and sister are particularly good for discussing the children; my husband and father more for work issues. When I am down I know I can talk to my husband and he will listen but his job is quite consuming and I don't always want to talk to him about something 'trivial' that may be bothering me. I suffered from postnatal depression after the birth of our second child and have learned not to keep my emotions in; better to tell others what is going on before it gets out of hand. It has taught me that there are a lot of things that could bring us down that really aren't worth getting upset about!

> 'My best friends play a HUGE role in keeping me going – they provide the adult talk and readjusting to normal when things are difficult at home. I try to set aside one evening per week to spend with friends. One friend visits occasionally from Germany and takes a lot of pressure off for a few days at a time.'

A Village to Raise a Child

As Hillary Clinton famously said, 'It takes a village to raise a child.' Given how disconnected we've become from that, I've been developing a utopian dream of co-operative domesticity. Imagine if we joined together with four other families and each cooked one weekday meal a week? Or if we shared caring for our kids and alleviated the stress of finding paid childcare? It's not so much an idyllic scene as a practical answer to many a working mother's gripe. If only we could break social constraints, get over any worries of being seen as weird or needy and invite others into our space. We've evolved to help one another, for goodness' sake; female kinship is central to our functioning. As Dr Louann Brizendine writes in her book *The Female Brain*:

As a rule, primates, including humans, are fairly practical about their investment in mothering. Many mother monkeys balance infant care with their essential 'work' of foraging, feeding activities and resting. They also pitch in when needed to care for offspring other than their own (alloparenting). An intriguing study of

> hunting among women of the Agta Negrito of Luzon underscores the functions of networks of female kin. Women's hunting has largely been regarded as biologically impractical because hunting is assumed to be incompatible with the obligations of infant care. Specifically, hunting forays were thought to impair women's abilities to nurse, care for, and carry children ... Agta women participate actively in hunting precisely because others are available to assume childcare responsibilities.

We can think we're alone or that we have to struggle on because everyone else is getting on with it, but the truth is many people are probably happy to help us out. And why not? Helping makes us feel good – we're hardwired for it – and relationships deepen when we're big enough to ask for or accept help. Mathilde, a good friend of mine, has no family nearby and being able to help her when she asks is good for both of us. I was once surprised by the gratitude she showed for the two hours I looked after her baby daughter when she went for a return-to-work meeting. Her thanks seemed disproportionate for the favour I'd done, and my thought is that it's because as a society we've lost touch with the idea of all mucking in together.

Friends and Family Making a Difference

Remember when you were a child and your best persuasion tactic involved the 'silent allies' approach to getting your own way? The 'everyone else has got one' plea and the 'but Katy's mum let's her' appeal? Although I know we're supposed to be more mature now, I don't think there's any harm in letting your family and friends know what help other working mothers have from theirs. If you don't ask you don't get – single mum Libby says she's learned that's the right attitude:

In theory there are lots of people who could help and some who I didn't even know would be happy to, but I guess it all comes to the asking and sometimes I'm not great at that either. It's a working mother 'I can do this on my own' pride thing. I have several amazing friends that I know I can call in a crisis (and do) and I feel very blessed by this.

> 'One of my grumbles about modern life is that the crucial family support network is missing for lots of parents. My wife is French and all her family live in Dijon and my parents are a two-hour drive away. Thankfully for us they are retired so have looked after our kids a fair bit, for which I'm always eternally grateful for otherwise we would have gone nuts a long time ago. However, this does tend to be say once every three months. Sometimes it would be nice when they are really driving you mad just to pick up the phone and say could you please pop over and look after them for a couple of hours? These tend to be the darker moments when you really need it!'

From swimming lessons and sewing to shopping and overnight stops, here's a flavour of what friends and families of some working mothers do to support them:

- 'I have a network of close friends with kids of similar ages who help provide that **companionship** on the long stretching weekends you have as a single mum. They give me things to look forward to and we enjoy that **shared parenting experience** together' (Rowan, mum)

- 'I pick up my three-year-old nephew from nursery, take him to his **swimming lesson** every Thursday and play for the rest of the afternoon until my sister is home' (Wendy, aunty)

- 'I'm 200 miles away from my grandchildren but I make school costumes, **sew** name badges in uniforms and **alter the kids' clothes** when I come to stay, to save my daughter-in-law the hassle' (Valerie, grandma)

- 'I take delivery of my neighbour's **grocery shopping** every week and put it away for her' (Jill, retired next door neighbour)

- 'I **pick up my friend's daughter** from the same morning nursery as my daughter on a Monday, Tuesday and Wednesday, and look after her for a couple of hours. My daughter enjoys the company and I feel good knowing that it helps my friend out.' (Diane, friend and mother).

- 'My neighbour and I take it in turns to **look after each other's boys** a couple of times a week when we're both back from work so one of us can go to a gym class/swim, as both our husbands don't get home until late' (Helen, friend and mother)

- 'My sister **looks after my son overnight** at the weekend once a month, which gives me some time off from the responsibility of being a single parent. Reece loves it because he gets spoiled, and I'll happily return the favour when she has children.' (Mandy, mum)

- 'My neighbour has two children the same age as my daughter and she looks after Alexandra from 7.30 a.m. on the mornings I have to leave early for work and **takes her to school**' (Srdjana, mum)

- 'My sister-in-law gives me all the **emotional support** I could ever need. She is wonderful, is in a similar position to me and understands my husband, which makes her advice invaluable' (Sheila, mum)

- 'My parents come and stay if I ask them to and feed us all and **fill up the fridge**' (Anna, mum)

- 'My mum and dad look after my youngest and pick my son up from nursery two days a week and generally **make an evening meal** for us on one of those days too. I do know I'm really lucky!' (Danielle, mum)

- 'My colleagues are amazing and their support is so valuable. I have friends there and my old head of group is **mentoring** me now. There is always someone to talk to and if I don't feel brave enough to ask, someone will always notice and ask me.' (Libby, mum)

- 'I collect my friend's children from the childminder, make dinner and **do the bedtime routine** once a month so she can stay late at work for a team meeting and drinks' (Liz, friend).

- 'I give my daughter the gift of **home-cooked meals in the freezer** every week! It's easy for me to make an extra portion of things like Bolognese or chilli, and I know it's a practical help to her' (Rachel, granny)

Kids Cutting Grass

Our three-year-old, Monty, is clearly not bored of hearing 'Mummy and Daddy are a team, I agree with Daddy' and 'Daddy and Mummy are a team, I agree with Mummy' because still he persists in trying it on with the other when one says no to biscuits at breakfast or telly before nursery. This being so, I'm always referencing our family as 'Team Chivers' in the hope that he will see it as an enviable thing to be part of – and it's working. He knows how to operate the vacuum cleaner, separate lights from darks before washing and, although I'm less keen to admit this for 'Health & Safety' reasons, can plug in the lawnmower and see to the grass.

Whilst I'm not advocating child labour (or slavery as my husband reminds me, since we're not actually paying him), I do think kids benefit from seeing the whole range of things that go into making family life harmonious and happy. And of course once you show them what they can and can't do yet to help, it can make them more keen to do so. To Monty's dismay I do draw the line at sharpening knives and power tools until he's at least seven – isn't that the age when psychologists say kids are capable of looking after themselves?!

Naturally, what you ask your kids to do depends on their age. Giving them a taste of self-responsibility can be as simple as asking them to tidy their toys away (from about age two) and building from there. Train them well and they'll give you many a smug moment at nursery parent consultations when Mrs Cowling tells you little Ronnie is the star helper *and* shows the other kids what to do. Or, if that's not important to you, think of the breakfasts in bed you can be enjoying by the time they're eight if you put the groundwork in now!

Ulrike has always had her kids involved in home-making:

Children need to feel part of a team, but understand you are the team leader. The key for us is that my children and I share housework, and they earn privileges such as going out by completing their chores.

My children understand that without me working, we wouldn't be able to afford the house, travel, school trips and lots more. They are, therefore, quite supportive.'

So what could your kids do to contribute? Go on, let your imagination run wild.

KEY IDEAS & ACTION POINTS

The working mum's mantra for this chapter is 'See your family as a team.'

- **Mindset**: Nearly 7 in 10 mothers say their partners believe that their going back to work is best for the family – so it's only right and reasonable that *the family* get involved in helping make your return to work, work.

- **Expectations**: Rethink your expectations about what it's possible for you to do at home once you're back at work. Wonder Woman is a character created by a man. She's not real.

- **Equality is an attitude**, not the act of dividing domestic chores down the middle. Be explicit with your partner about how you think you can both combine work and home life and appreciate the work you both put into family life (which can admittedly be a challenge at times).

- **Partners**: If your partner is reluctant to see the two of you as a team, consider things from his perspective to see how you can make a helpful difference to his mindset. Share your motivation for going back to work, and play up the positives that will interest him.

- **Friends and family**: Consider the friends and family around you who could help, and sound them out. If you're reluctant to ask, think about how you could make it a win-win, and about the difference it could make to your life and the kids – a happy mother equals a happy home.

MUM'S MANTRA

4

Find Childcare that Fits Your Family

Exploring, organizing and feeling confident about the childcare you choose.

If there were no schools to take the children away from home part of the time, the insane asylums would be filled with mothers.

Edgar W. Howe

Let's be honest: perfect childcare doesn't exist. Mary Poppins was a fictional *creation* who by today's standards would be struck off. Childcare is one of the biggest headaches that working parents face, and as far as I know there's no medicine to remedy it. However, with a decent dose of thought, planning and open-mindedness on your part, coupled with the collective wisdom of the parents in this chapter, finding childcare that fits your family needn't give you a pain.

Childcare that 'fits' your family means taking into account the needs and preferences of you and your partner, your child and any siblings. It's no good hiring a nanny because you think it's the best thing for baby if you work from home and will struggle to get anything done with them in the house. And it's pointless choosing a nursery close to home because its caring atmosphere assuages your guilt, if your commute means you'll be close to meltdown to make it back for pick-up time.

So how will you work out what childcare fits your family?

TUNE IN TO WHAT'S RIGHT FOR YOU

I've set about helping you work out what's best for your family by outlining the most common childcare options according to the experiences of real parents. Under each you'll get a picture of what it's like opting for that choice, to help you decide whether, on balance, it's a sound solution for your family. What *you* see as a benefit might be a drawback for another mum, which is why I haven't gone the route of pros and cons – that's for you to decide. For instance, one set of parents might choose a nanny because she provides one-to-one care for their child, similar to what the child would get from them, whereas others say that's exactly why they *don't* want a nanny. As this mum reflects:

> I couldn't bear Violet having more of a bond with a nanny than me because I have to work five days a week so the nanny would spend more time with her than me. In a nursery I know she's getting excellent care – there is a low staff turnover there – and she gets to play with lots of other children, which she doesn't get at home.

The second half of this chapter focuses on what parents say are 'Must Ask' questions to put to your child's potential care-provider, and solutions to common childcare stresses.

BE OPEN-MINDED

Before delving into what's on offer, let me suggest you read this chapter with a totally open mind. That means no skipping the nanny section because you think they're just for posh people, or poo-pooing nurseries or childminders because you've watched a distressing undercover exposé on the telly. As you're reading, it might be worth considering whether, like many mums, combining different options could suit you – some time with grandparents or your partner and other days in a nursery, for example. Depending on what stage you're at, it might be worth rereading this chapter after baby is born, as your feelings can change once you know your love bundle.

> *'Make sure you are really happy with your childcare arrangements, as it is so much easier to go back to work knowing your child is safe and happy and not having to worry about them. Allow plenty of settling-in time so you both get used to it.'*

A CHILDMINDER

From the age of six months both of my own children have been cared for by a husband-and-wife childminding team rated 'outstanding' by Ofsted. In 2010 there were 57,732 registered childminders doing 62 per cent of all childcare in England; of these, 9 per cent are graded 'outstanding' (quarterly Ofsted figures March 2010). I chose this *type* of childcare with my head, and the *individuals* themselves with my heart. Logically a nursery or a nanny wouldn't do because my work isn't regular and I couldn't afford (and didn't want) full-time childcare. By the time my son was a year old I'd picked up a lot of my corporate coaching work again and could be asked to do something in Birmingham on a Thursday one week or an overnighter in Guernsey the next. But then there might be nothing the week after and I would work on writing projects at home in the evenings. The solution lay with childminders who could offer a degree of flexibility, and fortunately for me there are several husband-and-wife childminding partnerships in my area. Single childminders may be able to offer flexibility, too, but with two minders working together they can look after a greater number of children – thereby offering the social stimulation I wanted Monty to have – and are often more open to flexible arrangements. We began with short core hours three days a week, and added more according to the work I was doing. Being with them 9–2 every Tuesday–Thursday gave my son consistency and ensured I always had some time each week to work one-to-one with private coaching clients.

> *'A childminder offers continuity of care (I've had some children stay with us for over 10 years) and offers the opportunity to experience the real world, i.e. going to the shops, the library, parks, etc. The children we look after enjoy the interaction with their peers, which is important for personal social and emotional development – they learn a lot from each other. Choosing a childminder means you are choosing someone with experience (having had their own children) and, nowadays, someone who is highly trained. Many have degrees in Childcare and Education.'*

Flexibility

Whilst childminders are usually a cheaper option than nurseries, in my case the trade-off for increased flexibility was a higher than average hourly rate (equivalent to the hourly rate for a nursery). This suited us fine as it was a big cost saving on the other option, which was to pay for three fixed days a week at a nursery when I might not have any work, and then the possible double-whammy of losing out on earnings if I was asked to do work on the two days we didn't have booked. It's worth adding that you should ask what the minder's hourly rate includes (nappies? meals? outings?), as a higher fee might be more cost-effective in the long run.

Childminders, like nurseries, usually charge for days when your child is off sick and when you go on holiday. Some childminders also expect to be paid during their holidays, whereas others, like the childminders we've used, don't charge for any of these things – what we use is what we pay for. It goes without saying that, while relevant, the cost of childcare shouldn't be the driver of your decision and there may be ways around prohibitively high costs (e.g. choosing a childminder closer to where you work, or organizing a nanny share).

What I really liked about the childminders we've used is their experience and the warm environment they have created for my children from babyhood; also that there's always been a positive male role-model for our boy. On paper they are 'outstanding' by Ofsted standards; what you can't necessarily put a grade on is the feeling of fun, care and warmth you get from a childminder or any caregiver. I trust them and feel confident about leaving my children in their care. I know what this mum means:

> I never fail to be amazed and overjoyed really to hear our childminder as excited about what our daughter has achieved or said as we are. It makes me so happy to hear that she is genuinely proud of our own daughter and has really enjoyed having her.

'If you can't afford a nanny at £300–£500 per week, then a childminder will be the much cheaper option. With no grandparents to help out, our childminder was perfect. She was a qualified nurse living in a house just like our own a stone's throw from us. It was really like an upmarket nursery.'

Home from Home

Another mum says:

> I love having a childminder. I took my son out of nursery as it wasn't working for me. I love him being in a home-from-home environment. He goes to playgroup, interacts with older kids and sleeps well there.

In a homely environment, where there are fewer children's needs to consider, your child is likely to be able to go for a nap at their preferred time and stick more closely to other aspects of their usual routine. However, as parents we have to be flexible and respect that the childminder has to consider the needs of other children in his or her care, too. It does our kids good to experience different ways of doing things, but if living by definite, unfaltering routine is important to you, be prepared for your search to take longer and the pool of people you pick from, smaller.

Another benefit of the childminders we've used has been the breadth and depth of their child-rearing experience, which not even the *Mumsnet* and *Netmums* forums have been able to rival at times. When I've wondered what to do about Monty haranguing his sister or how to succeed with potty–training, they've made suggestions based on what they've known to work and, crucially, what *my* children are likely to respond well to. I realize this is to be treasured and isn't something that necessarily comes with all childcare when I hear other mums comment on the youth of nursery staff and nannies.

'Our childminder gives our daughter more one–to–one care and attention than the nursery we use. She's in a home environment where she feels safe and happy, and she can be quite clingy, but going to the childminder has helped her through this in a big way. The nursery allows her to mix with other children of a wider age range and gives her greater independence. She is able to make decisions for herself and has to adapt and go along with what others are doing sometimes. The nursery cannot always be as flexible as the childminder and this helps her learn that sometimes plans can't be changed.'

With this knowledge and closeness to your child there sometimes comes a concern that baby will grow too attached to his or her carer, favouring them over you. In her thoughtful and thorough book *The Parent's Guide to Choosing Childcare*, Allison Lee allays this fear:

Many parents returning to work dismiss the idea of a one-to-one carer for their child purely for this reason, opting instead for a larger nursery setting where their child is less likely to form an intimate bond with a member of staff. Most nannies and childminders will tell you that they are not trying to be surrogate mothers to the children in their care, and many will go out of their way to reassure you ... I am a childminder myself. I am also a mother. Although I care greatly for the children in my care I have never wished to take the place of their parents and my feelings towards these children are very different from those I have for my own two sons.

Finding a Childminder that Fits Your Family

Your local Family Information Service (find it via www.childcarelink.gov.uk) can give you a list of childminders in your area, and you can view a childminder's latest Ofsted report at www.ofsted.gov.uk. Details of childminder availability are not always up to date on the Childcare Link website, so do phone to check as you may be pleasantly surprised or disappointed if you go to view then find out they can't accommodate your needs. A well-organized childminder will have a folder of registration documents, achievements, references and, perhaps most importantly of all, thank-you cards and testimonials you can flick through. Reading what other parents say about them can indicate the minder's particular strengths and whether they are right for your family.

Outstanding Ofsted-rated childminder Yvonne Purser says the acid test is whether you feel relaxed and happy when you leave your children in the minder's care:

> I encourage parents to ask whatever they like, and although the questions are usually fairly standard – what activities we do, attitude to discipline, mealtimes and opportunity for sleep – there are often a couple which are particular to that parent and which show what's important to them. It's answering those that can give the parents the feeling that you're right for them.

A NANNY

Nannies provide one-to-one care for your child in your home. Whilst there's no legal requirement for nannies to have formal childcare qualifications, many do and they usually have significant practical experience. Being an unregulated occupation there are no reliable statistics on how many nannies are operating in the UK. What we do know is that about 7,000 nannies are Ofsted-registered – but, according to Tricia Pritchard of Voice: The Union for Education Professionals, this doesn't tell parents anything meaningful:

> Ofsted registration for nannies is purely to enable parents to use childcare vouchers, and nannies only go on the voluntary part of the childcare register. A nanny being on this is not a measure of the standard of childcare and doesn't include the inspections childminders and nurseries receive.

Ofsted

At present there is no legal requirement for nannies to be Ofsted-registered, but if your nanny isn't you won't be able to claim the childcare element of Working Tax Credit or use employer-supported childcare vouchers. Some parents ask their nanny to register (this costs £100 in 2010, and includes a Criminal Records Bureau [CRB] check), perhaps offering to split the cost 50/50 or negotiate otherwise.

Nannies are cost-effective if you have two or more children or another family to share with. The hourly cost compares favourably with nurseries and childminders. According to the annual NannyTax (nanny payroll service) wage survey, in 2009 a nanny outside London cost on average £22,220 per annum gross, which works out at about £85 a day including four weeks' holiday pay. Central London nannies cost on average £32,316 (£124/day); outer London nannies £25,842 per year (£100/day) gross. Assuming an 11-hour day, that's £7.73, £11.28 and £9.09 per hour respectively. To put a positive spin on what may seem like eye-watering amounts, this means that when your children reach school age you're going to feel comparatively wealthy indeed.

Being Your Nanny's Employer

Whilst a nanny is the most cost-effective childcare option for many families, remember that hiring a nanny makes you her *employer*, which means **you** are responsible for paying her tax (hence the gross figures above) and National Insurance contributions. Obviously this significantly bumps up the cost and the hassle factor if you choose to do payroll duties yourself. However, many parents pay for the services of a company like NannyTax (www.nannytax.co.uk) to take away the stress.

Whatever stress the money side may bring, however, rest assured that a nanny can take a lot of early morning and evening stress away. Little Lottie can stay playing in pyjamas as you leave for work, and never will she be that last tear-stained babe to be collected from nursery if you were to get stuck in a jam on your way home. (And never will you be saddled with the horrendous late penalty fees I've heard nursery mothers talk of).

This mum extols the benefits of hiring a nanny:

I used to have a childminder, however my bill would go up and down; with the nanny I pay the same amount of money whether she is looking after one of them or all three of them. A nanny works so much better for us because the children are looked after in their own home, dinners are all cooked for them before I get back so when I walk through the door it is quality time with them.

'The only niggle I have with our nanny is that, by her own admission, she isn't the best cook and so I have to be a bit more organized with food. My children were familiar with my nanny before she started nannying for me so I felt better knowing her in advance rather than interviewing for the right person.'

A Personal Service

Most nannies will wash and iron your children's clothes as well as make home-cooked meals. They may do more – you have to ask and negotiate. Some families want this, others don't. One mum who chose a nanny-share for her second child told me how she balked at the nanny's suggestion that she could have her daughter 'fed, watered, bathed and ready for bed' when she came home. She and her husband felt strongly that these activities are things to be enjoyed, not something they want a nanny to do. And that's the beauty of a nanny – it's easy to highly personalize the 'service'.

A nanny has the freedom (compared to a childminder or nursery) to arrange activities and outings to suit your child, and can adjust plans more easily. You may have preferences for activities or groups you would like her to take your child to, and most nannies will happily accommodate your wishes. Depending on her knowledge of the area she may be able to suggest outings and experiences you might not have thought of, so do be open-minded and trust your nanny's judgement. If you're new to a neighbourhood, finding an established nanny with good local links could be important to you – and could be a question you want to ask (more on questions later in this chapter). Remember that you are responsible for paying for any activities or equipment your child needs, so that's something else to consider when you're weighing up the costs.

> 'When interviewing a potential nanny, give her some hypothetical problems and ask what she has done when faced with this sort of thing in the past. I've found my most successful childcarers have been big sisters with several younger siblings!'

Avoiding Days Off Work with a Sick Child

Whilst I'm not advocating leaving your child if he or she is downright poorly, many mums complain they get called away from work by nurseries when their child is fine apart from having a runny nose or mild cough. Nurseries tend to be very cautious about illness and naturally if your child has something like chicken pox then he or she definitely won't be able to attend. Most nannies on the other hand will be happy to crack on with caring for your little one whilst the spots scab over. Given that your children are likely to form a close bond with the nanny it's more likely they would be happy to continue to be cared for her even when they are feeling off-colour. And because they are cared for at home it's easy for a nanny to create a restful environment in which your children can get better. It's that home care, and one less change to cope with, which some mums say they like so much about hiring a nanny.

How to Find a Nanny

Unlike nurseries and childminders there's no central website for finding nannies in your area, although local nanny agencies can be found easily on the internet. Many mums say the best way is to put your feelers out at playgroups, postnatal groups, baby classes and in the doctors' waiting room. Ask, ask, ask and you will find, particularly at activity groups where you might be able to plug directly into the nanny network itself. I never realized how many of the people I thought were other parents were actually nannies at Wednesday morning *Hot Tots*!

A NURSERY

As with a nanny or a childminder, many parents exploring nursery care find personal recommendation one of the best ways of helping them choose. Founder of *Little Nightingales* nursery in Hertfordshire, Elena Journet, says 80 per cent of her nursery's places are filled by word of mouth and she regularly has disappointed parents who can't get a place. What may be surprising is *Little Nightingales'* 'satisfactory' Ofsted rating, but, as Elena explains:

It's standard practice for Ofsted to give a new childcare provider this rating on the first inspection and we're hoping for or a 'good' or 'outstanding' next time. Ofsted reports are great for giving detailed information about a nursery and I encourage parents to read them, but there's no substitute for word-of-mouth recommendation.

'What "sealed the deal" for me was how happy all the babies and kids were when I visited. There is regular communication on how my child is progressing and frequent parents' evenings. The nursery is also keen to engage with parents, and I am one of the three parent representatives on the nursery–parent liaison group. We meet quarterly to discuss any suggestions made by parents or any other relevant issues such as the Ofsted report or changes to policies. The staff are very amenable to parent requests and the management very approachable and flexible. Another bonus is that the nursery is open from 7 a.m. to 7 p.m. (as they cater for hospital/NHS staff who may have early starts or long shifts) and, unlike most nurseries, do not automatically charge you a penalty if you are occasionally a few minutes late.'

Ofsted inspections between 1 September 2008 and 31 March 2010 led to overall effectiveness gradings for childcare on non-domestic premises (i.e. nurseries) as follows: 10 per cent outstanding, 59 per cent good, 28 per cent satisfactory and 3 per cent inadequate. Childminder gradings were 9 per cent outstanding, 57 per cent good, 31 per cent satisfactory and 3 per cent inadequate.

Visit Several Settings to Compare

What one family may like might not appeal to you, so visiting a handful of nurseries before you make up your mind is always a good idea. By comparing facilities, routines, staff and the intangible 'feel' of a nursery you can be confident you have made the right choice. You might want to make a couple of visits and time these so you see different slices of the day before you decide. Even then, a 'final' choice can be changed if your child doesn't seem to be settling well after some trial sessions. Remember, childcare which both you and your child are happy with is crucial for a smooth return to work, and that's why settling your child into the new routine three or four weeks before you go back can mean less stress for everyone. More on this in the Mantra 7 chapter Prepare for a Smooth Return.

> *'I was very apprehensive about my son starting nursery and he was in an established routine so I wanted to ensure that this was not disrupted. I discussed his routine with his allocated key worker and every effort was made by her to accommodate this and any other wishes I had. We had "settling in" sessions which I found very reassuring and knowing my son was in an environment that he enjoyed and was well looked after certainly relieved a good deal of my stress.'*

But what should you be looking for in a nursery? And how do you know if a nursery is right for you?

It's the Carers Who Count

Parents and nursery managers agree that choosing a nursery over other forms of care is down to personal choice. Most parents decide to explore one form of care only, which is pragmatic given that investigating nurseries, nannies and childminders would be time-consuming and too many options could put your head in a spin. However, like parents and childcare professionals, I'm sure you'd agree that it's the people who care for our children who make or break a particular childcare option. So if you have the opportunity to explore a good handful of the people/places that you're hearing rave reviews about – regardless of whether that means a nanny, nursery or minder – you might find an excellent solution which you weren't necessarily expecting. Sue says she realized quality of care was more important than anything else, and chose her nursery on gut feel:

> Although I disliked the nursery near my work the first time I visited as it looked a little down at heel, I adjusted my criteria and realized that it should be judged on how the children are cared for and whether they are safe and happy rather than the building itself. I ended up preferring this nursery to my local one as I felt that the staff were kinder and more caring towards the children

> 'To me the most important thing is to walk around and see whether the staff are engaged with the kids and whether the kids look like they are enjoying themselves. If they can't get this right in front of visitors, it is not a great sign! Also, ask about how they communicate with parents – daily diaries are ideal, but there should also be regular parents' evenings so you get more time to discuss your child than you would at pick-up time.'

Developmental psychology has shown us that infants need to form secure emotional attachments to the people who care for them. In nurseries where there's a high staff turnover this may not be possible, and that's why asking about this – and about what a nursery does to motivate, develop and retain employees – is important.

Key Workers

In a nursery environment your child will be allocated a 'key worker', and it's this person who will record what your child has done each day and whom you should chat to in the first instance about any queries or niggles you have. Although parents value the key-worker system, many say it's the team of care that attracts them to using a nursery. As this mum puts it:

> I did an 'organizational behaviour and management' course at university and decided that a well-run nursery might be better able to support a carer when he or she is having an off day; you can't get that from a sole carer (such as a nanny or childminder).

A team approach to care also means your child gets to meet and learn from different people as well as the added benefit that, unlike with a nanny or childminder, if your key worker is ill, your childcare isn't affected. This may be particularly important to you if you'd really struggle to arrange a back-up care plan, as this mum says:

> I chose full-time nursery over a childminder because of the age of my children (two and three) and the fact that, having no back-up in terms of close family, it is vital that I am not let down by illnesses, holidays, etc. As our local nursery was full on Tuesdays, Wednesdays and Thursdays, I chose a nursery near my work for those days. Two different nurseries was not ideal for my children, but it was the best (and most financially viable) choice out of my options. A nanny two days a week would have been ideal, but tax, employer's liability, etc. made that financially impossible.

Qualifications

Nurseries separate children according to age/developmental stage, which means they are among their peers and benefit from appropriate activities and toys. As with childminders, nurseries have different children-to-carer ratios depending on age, so it's important to take into account the staffing levels, qualifications and years of experience when making a decision. Currently the law here in the UK says there must be at least one member of staff for every three children under age two, and at least one member of staff must hold a full and relevant Level 3 Diploma for the Children & Young Person's Workforce (as set out by the Children's Workforce Development Council – an executive non-departmental public body sponsored by the Department for Education), as well as having suitable experience of working with children under two.

'My god-daughters still talk about the nursery they attended, and you can't get a better recommendation than that, so we chose it when it was time to find somewhere for our daughter. It's in a great location, on the way to/from work for both me and my hubby. When we went round it was noisy, the kids were having fun and were alert and interested in meeting our daughter. It didn't have all the equipment some nurseries have, but the staff made it: they were so interested in the kids and they remembered me picking up my godchildren and asked after them by name three years on.'

The qualifications staff hold can be a good indicator of individual staff members' commitment to the work they do and the attitude of the nursery to their employees' development. Early Years Professional Status (EYPS) is the gold standard for those working with children under the age of five according to the CWDC but it isn't a legal requirement and only

4,000 people working with children in the UK currently hold it.

AN AU PAIR

When my children were three and one, a German au pair came to us out of the blue (a long story). I was stoked at the prospect of having an extra pair of hands, and naturally we met before welcoming her into the family. However – and this really does bring home the message of meeting a few different childminders/nannies/au pairs/nurseries before you make your mind up – it became clear within the first month that there wasn't going to be a big love-in going on between her and my kids. I would probably have turned her down if I'd met other au pairs to compare her to, and this is purely because I don't think she fitted in with our family. Yes she was competent, yes she was kind and polite, yes she could do the chores I asked of her. She was a great conversationalist, bright, cultured and thoughtful – *but* there was no natural affinity with my kids. This caused me anguish, guilt and an almost constant feeling of physical tension in my body, particularly in the last few weeks of her stay. My son was reluctant to go out of the house with her and even took to his bed one afternoon after nursery instead of playing with her. This left me feeling all sorts of things: sad for my boy, cross that she couldn't be more appealing to my children, annoyed that I was carrying this constant stress around with me, and bad at the thought that my son's rejection might dent *her* self-esteem.

Having said all this, au pairs can be a great source of support, particularly in families where one parent works long hours or you have early starts, late finishes or shift patterns. As Anna says:

with four children under six and a husband away all week, an au pair has been life-saving, along with nursery on the days I work. She lives in and needs to be looked after, but is a great support/friend.

One of the big motivators for taking our au pair on was to bridge an early morning childcare gap when I was joining my husband in a ridiculously early commute two days a week. The alternative, had she not been with us, would have been for my husband to set off later, use the childminder for an extra hour and miss family time in the evenings as he would have had to stay later at the office. I'm fortunate that if we hadn't had an au pair we could have run this scenario if need be; for some families that wouldn't be possible. This is but one example of the gazillion trade-offs and compromises families with young children make every day.

'My husband and I have demanding full-time jobs. Our kids are in their teens now and we've had 11 au pairs since they were little. Roughly one-third were excellent, a third OK and a third downright awful. When your kids are really young it might seem like a hassle but finding separate people to cover what you need doing (e.g. cleaner for housework, good childminder/nanny for care, someone to do the ironing and a reliable, trustworthy babysitter for nights out) is better than trying to roll it all into one and hoping you get the perfect au pair to do it. An au pair is great when the kids are in school for after-school pick-ups and running them to after-school clubs, ferrying to their friends' houses, etc.'

Not a Nanny Substitute

Our au pair was confident about being left with our children for the morning routine twice a week, but an au pair is not a substitute for other forms of childcare for long stretches of time. Especially in families with very young children, an au pair is best thought of as an extra pair of hands. Given that I do a lot of work from home my vision was for the children to play merrily with Julia in the garden, bake buns in the kitchen and create lots of wonderful things with Lego, paper, paint and glue anywhere but where I was working. Given what I've already told you, it probably isn't a surprise to learn it didn't quite happen like this! Although a lot of creative endeavours went on, they often involved me, too.

Finding an Au Pair that Fits Your Family

Seasoned au pair-hirer Allison recommends placing or responding to adverts on www.gumtree.com to find someone who's already in the country whom you can interview face to face before saying yea or nay. Tara, mum of three, recommends asking lots about a prospective au pair's family life: 'An au pair who is herself an older child with lots of younger siblings has been a good bet in my experience.'

FAMILY

From au pairs to animals – no, I don't mean dog-as-baby-sitter as per *Peter Pan* or anything else highly dangerous or illegal ... I'm sure just about every family in the UK has owned a copy of Eric Carle's *The Very Hungry Caterpillar*. But the book you really need by Mr Carle right now is *Mister Seahorse*. It's packed with examples of fish species where dad plays a proactive parenting role, and as a bedtime story it's a great warm-up to downstairs discussions of childcare and your partner's involvement in it.

The vast majority of women I've surveyed say organizing childcare falls to them alone (83 per cent in my survey) and the idea of their partner staying at home to care for their children meets with a 'you must be joking' face. However, I've met several dads who do it. IT contractor Asim is just one of them, and explains how it works for his family:

Having three children of various ages means that juggling full-time work between us isn't always easy. However I think we've adapted to it because we had children young and don't really know life without them. I work on a 3 p.m.–midnight shift, with an on-call week monthly. Amina tends to work long days as a midwife either from 7 or 8 a.m. twice a week, with a night shift on a Sunday so she can be back home in time to see the kids to school. Amina went back to work when our youngest, Adam, was 18 months old and for the first time I took on the majority of the childcare during the day. It's hard, tiring, thankless work – but I also enjoy it and I've finally come to understand a little of what Amina meant when she used to say that these few years are precious. I've come to know and understand Adam in a way that I maybe didn't with the girls and feel very privileged for that.

'I work sporadic hours so need flexibility, which I found only my mother could do without a drama! I class myself as a protective mother and found the whole idea of giving my daughter over to someone I barely know very scary. I know 100 per cent that my child is loved, cared for and adored by my parents and they put her needs first in any given situation. My mother is an extended version of me to my daughter, and if she is upset she will sometimes ask for my mum's support rather than mine. If that was another carer I think I could get quite upset knowing my daughter chose them over me to pacify her.'

Where a partner's involvement is not a workable solution you'll benefit as a family from at least sharing the selection and organization load that goes with childcare – be that doing drop-offs or pick-ups, vetting nanny CVs or paying the nursery fees. Remember, think like a team for the good of the family.

Beyond the two of you, who else could help? Grandparents, an uncle, a sister-in-law?

According to the charity *Grandparents Plus*, one in three working mothers relies on grandparents for childcare. Many of the grandmas and granddads I've chatted to say it's a privilege and they enjoy taking care of their grandchildren. Doreen and Michael have looked after their two sets of grandchildren since they were babies, and explain how all benefit:

> We look after our daughter's two children one day a week and our son's children on another day. That time is special and we're very close because of it. It keeps us young, not to mention making our daughter's life easier. One day with each of our grandchildren feels right, as it feels like a treat. It's enough to be fun and not too much that we get tired or feel taken for granted. I don't want to play the nagging mother role again!

Sam also has the help of her mum one day a week:

> I work four days a week. My daughter (20 months old) goes to nursery three days a week and stays with one of her grandmas on the fourth day. We wanted her to go to nursery on the other days to give her a variety of developmental opportunities in a structured environment.

I also believe that being in a busy environment with a number of other children will encourage her social skills and will make starting school less of a shock. To be honest, we didn't want to burden the grandparents with regular childcare responsibilities either, but we had to ask because of the cost of nursery. The fees are only marginally less for four days a week than if she were there full-time. However, by dropping down to three days of nursery the costs were more pro-rated.

As Sam alludes to, grandparental care may work best when it's blended with another form of care. One grandma, Margaret, said she doesn't think her daughter realizes how tiring she finds looking after her granddaughter, and that scaling back to one or two days a week would be perfect. She says, though, that she knows this would make things difficult financially and practically for her daughter. Other family carers I've spoken to about how to make 'family as childcare' work say they don't want or expect money, just appreciation and acknowledgement. And this is probably the main niggle with using family: not knowing quite where the boundaries are, and the lack of a clear-cut business-like relationship. When we entrust our children to paid care with clear policies and expectations we know where we stand. But isn't that just the very nature of using childcare – pros, cons, benefits and drawbacks every which way you turn?

I said at the beginning of this chapter that there's no such thing as perfect childcare, only a best fit for your family. You might find the following activity useful for picking over the different avenues available and coming up with a picture of what looks best for yours.

Exercise ✏

Thinking about the various different childcare possibilities, divide a sheet of paper into four boxes and label them Nanny, Childminder, Nursery, Family. (Yes, I know I've left out au pairs – this is because I don't feel you should think of an au pair as a long-term childcare solution, necessarily.) In each one write down why it could be a positive choice for your family. Think about it from your own perspective and your child's – how could each option be good for you, and what would your child potentially like about it? This exercise may be a test of open-mindedness depending on your pre-existing views of childminders, nannies and nurseries.

QUESTIONS TO ASK

Nurseries, nannies and childminders will expect you to have lots of questions, so feel confident about reeling them off. Below are the top questions the working parents I surveyed think are important to ask. You might find it helpful to ask preliminary questions over the phone (one and two on the list as a minimum) and from the answers to those decide whom to shortlist for a face-to-face interview.

Ofsted reports can be downloaded for free from www.ofsted.gov.uk to read before interviewing a nanny or going to visit a childminder or nursery.

The Basic 10

1. **Do you have space for my child and from what date?**

2. **How much are your fees and what do they cover?**

3. **What would my child do on a typical day?**

4. How much time do you spend talking and engaging with the children and how?

5. What sort of food and snacks do you provide?

6. Where would my child sleep and can my child sleep when he or she needs to?

7. What's your policy on discipline and how do you manage behaviour?

8. How do you help children feel settled and deal with anxiety or crying?

9. What help are you able to offer when potty-training?

10. How will you 'hand over' at the end of the day?

> *'I think you just get a feeling about a person/nursery – a bit like when you go looking at houses to buy. If looking for another nursery or nanny I would ask more questions about disciplining and activities.'*

Childminder-specific Questions

1. How many years have you been caring for children and what ages have you looked after?

2. How many children are you registered to care for?

3. How many children do you currently have and what's the gender and age mix?

4. Where do the children play? (e.g. safe, clean playroom and outdoor area)

5. How would you incorporate my child's preferred routine with the other children's?

6. What outings, activities and playgroups do you get involved in?

7. Do they watch TV or DVDs?

8. Do you meet with other childminders for trips out?

Nanny-specific Questions

1. What experience do you have as a nanny? Have you any qualifications?

2. Why are you leaving your current family?

3. If nannying for more than one child, how do you deal with different ages?

4. How would you deal with X scenario?

5. What are your holiday plans for the year ahead?

6. How long are you happy to commit to us?

Nursery-specific Questions

1. How many members of staff have left in the last year? Reasons?

2. What qualifications does your team hold? Experience?

3. Who would be looking after my child and what experience and qualifications does he or she have?

4. What's your policy on child illness?

5. What outdoor provision do you have for my child?

6. Is there scope for dropping off early or picking up late?

7. Are there additional activities offered and at what cost? What will my child do if not taking part?

8. How easy is it to get hold of someone during the day if I

want to check on my child? Is it possible to contact you by email so that my whole office doesn't hear me calling?

9. What will you do if my child doesn't want to come in?

Exercise

Your Personalized Question List

Thinking about your child, your situation and your values, what is it important for you to know about any potential childcare provider in order to make an informed decision? Write down your questions on a blank sheet of paper. When you have finished, reread each question and think about what you ideally want to hear from any potential nursery, childminder or nanny when you ask it. This will help you get clear about what you are looking for, and may help you to rule a provider in or out more quickly when you meet.

CHILDCARE STRESSES AND WHAT TO DO ABOUT THEM

Even the happiest of childcare arrangements get interrupted with stresses from time to time. Here are some suggestions from working mums on how they've handled five of the most common ones.

> *Stress:* I thought I'd been organized but I've left childcare too late.
>
> *Soother:* Incredibly, some mums get their unborn baby's name down as soon as they see that thin blue line. If you haven't, never fear; childcare has a way of working itself out, as Beth says:

149

I can honestly say don't panic! I was getting really stressed and then my son got a place at the nursery I wanted with just four weeks' notice. Although nurseries have long waiting lists, children do leave unexpectedly and only need to give a month's notice. I was the only person on their nine-month waiting list who needed a place so soon and therefore got the place. Do check out nannies and childminders, too, to spread your net as wide as possible, and it will come good.

'It doesn't matter what you ask them, it is what the other parents say. Always try and go for recommendations.'

Alternatively you could talk to your employer about delaying your return, or organize interim care as Becky did whilst waiting for her first choice to be free:

I got an unexpected job offer and had to start four weeks before our nanny share could be up and running. A friend covered one week, my husband took annual leave for one and each set of grandparents had the boys for the remaining two weeks, which was great as my husband and I were footloose and fancy-free in the evenings – a real treat!

Stress: Getting called back to nursery for a poorly child.

I surveyed 150 working mothers and just 5 per cent said that if their child were to be taken ill during the day it would be Dad who came to collect baby. Illness can be a big headache, as Stephanie says:

whilst I love being back, one of the big challenges I am having is the seemingly continual need to take time off to look after my baby when he is unwell. I have chosen to put him into a nursery for the interaction with other babies, and knew in the back of my mind that being with other children would also expose him to lots of germs and bugs.

Soother: Ask your potential childcare provider what their policy is on illness, and let them know your preferred way of handling it. As Teresa writes:

I had to use two nurseries. I was really pleased with both, but they had different policies on what to do when a child is ill. Nursery A's clientele were mainly working mums and the nursery would do all that they could to prevent the parent having to pick the child up early. For example, they would give Calpol to bring temperatures down and put the child in a quiet room. Nursery B was located in a wealthy area where it was used mainly to give non-working mums a day off from the kids. Their policy was to send children home as soon as they got a temperature. As a working mum who didn't want to come across as flaky to her employers, Nursery A was the better option as it meant less chance of having to leave work early.

And Karen says:

When a child starts at a nursery, they inevitably pick up every bug going and spend a month going from one cold/stomach bug to another. I was prepared for it second time around and deliberately took my daughter to crèches and playgroups before starting at nursery to give her a chance to mingle with other germs!

Stress: My childcare's temporarily fallen through.

Soother: There are likely to be times when your child is not so poorly you judge you need to stay at home but he's not well enough to (or still contagious so can't) go back to nursery or the childminder. For this reason it's worth while preparing some contingency plans before you need them. A friend, neighbour or family member usually fits the bill, or if that's not possible sow the seed at work of working from home (if your job permits) when days like these happen. These same plans come in handy should your childcare fail due to the carer's sickness, holiday or snow closure, for instance.

Stress: I'm worried about my child not settling into the childcare we've organized.

Soother: Children are adaptable little things and in most cases when you disappear so does the blotchy red face and weeping (and so should yours – you know she's in good hands). As well as being signs of upset, tears and clinginess are our children's mechanisms for keeping us close, and when you're not there they serve no purpose. As Stephanie recalls:

On day two of my son's settling-in period he was extremely upset and in tears (he was just over 12

152

months old). This made me very upset as well. The staff took Jack off me (he was hanging on for dear life) and told me to leave. Tough but fair, and what I needed. The real positive spin was that about 30 minutes later the nursery called me to reassure me that he had settled down fine and was happily playing with the other children and toys. It was such a nice and reassuring thing to do and put my mind at rest.

Stress: There seems to be an endless string of little niggles with our childcare.

Soother: If the care you've chosen isn't working out as you expected, it could be that you've made some (wrong) assumptions or that for whatever reason your expectations are out of sync with your provider's. So many problems can be resolved by talking things through early on and thinking about whether overall you're happy with the care. Try saying things like 'I think *I* may have misunderstood about what the children will eat at lunch ...' instead of the accusative '*You* haven't been feeding my child properly.' A constructive conversation will keep the relationship intact. As Pam says:

We have had a few problems with the continuity of our son's key worker and sometimes communication is not quite up to scratch – we just raise any issues with the manager and things tend to get worked out reasonably quickly.

That said, there are undoubtedly times when it's not about resolution but a radical childcare rethink.

You can't quantify emotions or intuition, but if yours are telling you the care isn't what you want then it may be better to change, for your own peace of mind. Laura moved her son from a nursery to a childminder:

I was unhappy with the admin staff at his nursery – they didn't answer the phone or reply to emails. When they failed to respond to my complaint, I took my son out of there. Although the women looking after him were great, I felt that he wasn't getting the overall care I wanted. I always tell people now that childcare is not set in stone, and if you're not happy, you can always change.

KEY IDEAS & ACTION POINTS

The working mum's mantra for this chapter is 'Find childcare that fits your family.'

- **Keep an open mind:** Consider all the options before narrowing your choices. The best 'fit' might be something unexpected.

- **Know what matters to you**: Listen to the wisdom of other parents, but ultimately consider your own values and needs when drawing up a list of questions to put to a potential provider.

- **Consider the pros and cons**: What might be a pro to you could be a con to another, so tune in to the benefits and drawbacks of a potential childcare solution from *your* family's perspective.

- **Go for personal recommendation**: If other parents are pleased, there's a good chance you will be. Keep your ear to the ground for hot places, nannies on the move and childminders worth their weight in gold.

- **Weigh up which options work best for the whole family**: Make your ultimate childcare choice based on what's going to work well for you, your partner and your child(ren).

MUM'S MANTRA

5

Get a Grip on Guilt

What is the point of maternal guilt? It's not a natural, bio-determined force with any benefit for children. It doesn't protect them from predators or improve their health. It's a wasted anxiety with historical roots stretching back a mere decade or two since the rise of the middle-class working mother.

LESLEY THOMAS, JOURNALIST

Do you know where your G-spot is? Every mother has one; every mother knows she has one – and boy, do we feel it when it's rubbed. I'm referring to your very real 'guilt spot', guilt being the second most frequently cited problem working mothers face – the first being finding good-quality, affordable childcare. I think the subject deserves a whole chapter on how to get a grip on it, if not get rid of it altogether.

All my own guilt tends to cluster around my kids' happiness or potential lack of it. Take this example: a couple of weeks after we'd welcomed an au pair into our home, I headed into London to give a talk about working mothers and guilt at The Vitality Show. As I tried to leave the house my son morphed into a cross between Bambi and a giant squid (big, doleful eyes and a tangle of arms and legs attempting to suck the life-force out of me), pleading in a tragic Shakespearean sort of way not to leave him. This being the third such episode that week, my G-spot was well and truly rubbed. What did I do? I remembered that kids can smell guilt (but not before dithering a bit, admittedly) and that any attempt to stay and try and settle him with 'I love you, I'll see you later, you'd better have a really fun morning or else there's no cake after tea' would be bad for both of us. I left the house with his blotchy face ghosting in my mind, and started to see the incident as bonus authentic fodder for my talk. And no, I *didn't* feel guilty about that.

It took a few weeks before Monty got used to me leaving the house (and him in the house with his sister and our au pair) but he did get used to it. My solution was to walk out the door before daddy left so *he* could deal with the histrionics. Of course daddy got none of it: no guilt pheromones in the air, I reckon. I also began to reflect that Monty's problem was not so much me leaving as being left with our houseguest/au pair. I reasoned that up until this point in his short life he'd only been cared for by bubbly people like me, and that maybe I was doing him a favour introducing him to other types of people. As mum-of-two Lisa says, 'Children need to learn from others as well as their family, and by entrusting them to other carers I think everyone appreciates one another more.'

SOCIALLY CONSTRUCTED GUILT

If you're anything like me or the 50 or so other mothers I canvassed on what makes them feel guilty, I expect you've had more than a pang of guilt about many things connected with going back to work. But where does guilt come from? And how best to deal with it?

I reckon a lot of guilt is socio-culturally determined. By that I mean we've learned to feel guilty, and the root of it is our constant comparisons with what other mothers are doing, or not doing. If we were all sailing in the same direction we'd probably be much more relaxed about going with the flow without any backward guilty glances. But because we've moved into a time of increased choice about how we mother – indeed, to a right-on age where we 'parent' rather than 'mother' – we can get caught up in a tangle of guilt-inducing comparisons with mothers who do things differently. I think more choice might have been bad for us. Psychologists studying the effects of greater or lesser choice have shown that, far from making us happier, having lots of options can make us feel less confident about our choices. This is because there are so many alternatives we worry we may regret not having chosen something else.

I've heard stay-at-home mothers talk about feeling guilty because they're not going back to work, or worrying they may be spoiling their kids by being too available to them. We're awash with guilt at every turn; damned if we do and damned if we don't. Rather than this being a negative state of affairs, I think we can turn it into a positive by logically nullifying it all. Let's say begone to guilt!

Lisa describes the potential for guilt whichever which way you turn:

I am currently not working as I have moved to Italy where I will be living for the next three years due to my husband's work. I now actually feel guilty for NOT working as I struggle to know how to entertain my two-year-old every day. I feel guilty in that it would actually be easier being at work, and at 40 years old my biggest fear now is getting a job when we return to the UK. I am currently trying to focus on how I can use the next few years to my advantage to improve my prospects of getting a worthwhile job when I get back. It's difficult with Pippa at home, but she will be going to nursery three days a week in a couple of months' time – and then I'll probably battle with feelings of guilt about that because I won't be working! It seems like a neverending battle of wits at the moment but I'll get there in the end.

On a similar positive note, Hayley reflects on how she's learned to handle guilt:

I had postnatal depression after our second child was born and felt immensely guilty that her first year of life was such a blur to me. However, the recovery from that enabled me to see that guilt is a natural (or at least a very common) feeling for mothers, working or not, and that I should accept those feelings but also keep them in context, not beat myself up about them or dwell on them. Deep down I know that I am a loving mother and that I do what I have to do for them as well as for me.

Lesley Thomas' opening quote for this chapter describes guilt as having no benefit to our kids – ergo, let's forget it and move on. I think she has a point – although, like pain, guilt *can* be a warning that something's wrong. As writer Fay Weldon once reflected:

No one likes to feel guilty. We tell ourselves we're entitled to do what we want to do and that guilt is merely the result of our upbringing. But I believe guilt is to the soul what pain is to the body: it indicates what we ought and ought not to be doing, and should be listened to.

THE GUILT HIERARCHY

Sadly for us, pain differs from guilt in that we can experience more than one guilt at a time (you experience only the greater pain in your body if there are a few competing ones. Hence when 37 weeks pregnant and almost paralysed by toothache I prayed for the onset of labour). Of course, though, some guilt grips us harder than others, and so I've attempted to order this chapter into a sort of 'hierarchy of guilt' according to what the 50 or so mums I've spoken to about it have said.

I agree that guilt can be a good barometer of whether the decisions we make are good or bad for us and our families. Guilt can be the voice that makes us stop and question our motives and change our ways for the better. We need to ask ourselves, 'Is this guilt that I'm feeling reshaping my feelings and actions for the better, or is it pointless and destructive?'

One of my own biggest sources of guilt used to be that I was not spending enough time playing with my children because I was prioritizing cleaning, cooking and emails above them. I perceived the guilt in this situation to have been a force for good because it made me stop and re-evaluate my priorities. It also made me see that I was putting too much pressure on myself to earn decent money without having the right amount of childcare in place to make it happen. I was trying to be an almost full-time mother and earn 75 per cent of what I did before kids, with not even two days' childcare a week. The guilt helped me see I was being ridiculous and needed to change. And I did.

On the other hand there's the unhealthy guilt that Jo experienced every week when she considered the length of time her daughter spent at nursery so she could work full-time in a job she enjoys. She went round the same guilty loop week after week without anything changing. There was nothing positive about these feelings and they undermined the enjoyment she got from her work. Things changed when she accepted she had a choice and that, given the other options, she would rather carry on working full-time than not work at all or move to a lower-status role. In a way it helped her to recognize that if she didn't work she wouldn't be able to pay the mortgage. Guilt's a luxury when you put it like that.

Starting with separating ourselves from our children – the most fundamental aspect of being a working mother – the rest of this chapter focuses on what working mothers say they feel most guilty about and how they get a grip on it. Let their experience stop guilt from getting a hold on you (and not become a breeding-ground for more guilt when you read about things you hadn't thought to feel guilty about before now).

GETTING A GRIP ON SEPARATION GUILT

It's no wonder you feel guilty when you separate from your child when you think of the clever, complex chemistry affecting your brain since before your baby was born. We're engineered to want to stay close to our children, although most of us admit, at least to ourselves, that we also love to be away from them. Louann Brizendine writes in *The Female Brain* about why it can be hard to leave our child:

> ... physical cues from the infant forge new neurochemical pathways in the brain that create and reinforce maternal brain circuits aided by chemical imprinting and huge increases in oxytocin. These changes result in a motivated, highly attentive, and aggressively protective brain that forces the new mother to alter her responses and priorities in life. The stakes are life and death. In modern society, where women are responsible for not only giving birth to children but working outside the home to support them economically, these changes in the brain create the most profound conflict of a mother's life.

MUM'S G-SPOT: Looking forward to time away from my kids

I feel guilty that I want to be a working mum, and it is a choice I make because I do not feel I could get the stimulation I need, or be a good mum, if I stayed at home. I feel guilty that I enjoy leaving them, enjoy work and adult company, and that I don't want to be a full-time mum. I also don't have to work, which makes me feel more guilty about leaving them. And I feel guilty if I am not in a fantastic mood on a Thursday or Friday when I don't work.

Sometimes I long for the ordered world of work when the children are playing up, and other times I feel guilt about the children preferring to spend time with carers other than me. I feel guilty that I should need a break from the children and actually enjoy my work because it gives me a break.

Guilt Gripped

Every mother I've spoken to who likes going out to work, yet feels guilty about doing so, says she just couldn't contemplate being at home full-time and that her kids are better off because she's balancing her needs with her kids'. Researchers Ylva Elvin-Nowak and Helene Thomsson, studying working mothers in Sweden, conclude that mothers who are both mentally and physically accessible to their children yet who find fulfilment beyond them (i.e. pursuing their chosen careers) promote their children's well-being. Like other researchers and psychologists, they are giving support to the 'happy mothers make happy children' model. That's something Becky agrees with:

I feel guilty that I leave my children with someone else to look after them and that I actually look forward to having three days a week which isn't about them. I keep telling myself it will benefit them if I have some time out. We will have better quality time together when I am at home, and hopefully I will feel a generally more rounded person by going back to work and therefore enjoy my time with them more because I appreciate it more.

Writing in the *Journal of Family and Marriage*, Jackie Guen-douzi says: 'For many women the workplace with its peer support and focus on the individual's identity may actually provide a less stressful environment than the home where the woman's identity is subsumed by the family role as mother.' When I have time away from my kids to do the work I love, I come back feeling refreshed and bountiful. Being with them constantly, relentlessly responding to their requests, I can feel resentful and subjugated – as Mathilde reminds herself when guilt creeps in about enjoying her work:

I try to remember that when I have them 24/7 I get annoyed and impatient, and that I am much better at spending quality time with them when I have had my own 'quality time'. I also repeat to myself, a lot, a happy mum makes a happy child.

There's only so much of meeting other people's needs we can do before wanting to get away from it. If you can work through in your own mind what's the optimum balance of time spent with and apart from your child, and you are able to achieve it, then logically speaking there's no reason to feel guilty during the time you're not available to them. Kids can never have enough of us, so even if they protest and cry when we leave them, it *is* important that you act on your own needs.

MUM'S G-SPOT: Separation anxiety

My son is very clingy and I blame the fact that he is scared to let me go as he does not know that I will come back. That makes me feel awful for not being able to give him the confidence in me he needs.

Guilt Gripped

Consistency of care seems to play a big part in easing the stress of separation, so consider how you can make this happen as part of your childcare arrangements. Check out the staff turnover rates in any nurseries you approach, or consider a nanny or a childminder if you're looking to find just the right person to nurture your child. Remember that kids are highly attuned to our emotions and if you seem confident and cheerful around the person or people that you are leaving your little one with, then that will help him, too.

To downplay her guilt on the separation issue, this mum focuses on how she spends more time *with* her son than without him:

I know I spend more quality time with my son than many mothers; we are always playing and exploring the world together. I spend hours just playing with him every day, but I do not do that to manage my guilt; I do it because I love it. Thinking rationally I know the clinginess will pass and as he gets older he'll understand when I'm going and when I'm coming back.

Louise offers this advice:

Children are very resilient and will cope better than you think. In a way it's making the children stronger, too, and they may not be so mothered and become more independent. They may seem clingy but when you're not around they're perfectly fine.

MUM'S G-SPOT: Not enough time playing with my child

- **Lee-Rose:** I feel guilty about not spending valuable time with the children but also knowing it would drive me nuts staying at home every day.

- **Amanda:** Guilt, gosh, where to start? ... Fitting in house-work with the few hours I have away from work, when I feel I should be spending valuable time with my son Alexander (18 months). I seem to spend so much of my time keeping on top of cleaning, washing, etc. I tell myself to just leave it, but it just builds up.

- **Audrey:** I feel guilty about not spending enough time with my child, not prioritizing him as much as I should and being on the phone all the time.

- **Claire:** I feel guilty about not having as much time for the minutiae of development in my second child versus when my first was smaller and not taking them to music, dancing and God knows what other classes like some parents do.

Guilt Gripped

- **Amanda:** Some of the time the guilt is self-imposed rather than the child actually being bothered. To manage my feelings of guilt, I tell myself that a lot of mothers need to work these days, just to pay the bills. The extra money gives us all as a family a better quality of life. I just try and make sure that the time I do have with my son is quality time. We have a great relationship, Alexander loves going to nursery and I believe the balance between nursery and home life gives him varied experiences.

- **Lee-Rose:** I know if I didn't go to work I would be in a bad mood most of the time – I need to have a break to come back to them with fresh energy so it is also better for them.

- **Claire:** I only work three days a week and try not to think about work too much on the days I'm with them. I reassure myself that they enjoy pre-school and the time they spend with their grandparents instead of me. I also play the 'at least I'm not as bad as that' game in my head when I see kids having tantrums in the street or babies eating crisps!

- **Audrey:** I put my gremlin in its place when it rears its ugly, ultra-critical head. I remind myself that a happy, fulfilled mum makes a happy, fulfilled child and I compare myself with other mums who work and remind myself that I actually spend loads of time with him and do prioritize him!

- **Hannah:** I try to schedule time out with the children, doing things that we all enjoy. We have started occasionally paying a babysitter during the day if there is something we need to do that the children would most definitely not enjoy (e.g. house-hunting). There is no point struggling on with things you have to do with small children wailing because you feel guilty handing them over to someone else. A bit of pragmatism goes a long way.

MUM'S G-SPOT: Giving up breastfeeding to go back to work

> I feel that breastfeeding is the best thing for my daughter and I have enjoyed doing it but now I feel selfish that I'm stopping to go back to work after seven months when I could take more time off and carry on with it.

Guilt Gripped

As so many of the women I've spoken to have said, being a mother is both wonderful and frustrating. One of the biggest frustrations is that every choice we make seems to be a trade-off, and so it is with the choice to give up breastfeeding. The UK Department of Health recommends breastfeeding exclusively for six months and, as Kirsty says, she's exceeded that:

> I know my daughter has had the best possible start in life, and probably if I stayed at home any longer I'd feel that I was missing out and maybe then the breastfeeding would feel less lovely. I tell myself that there will never be a perfect time to stop and that I'd be facing the same thoughts if I stayed off work for another month or however long.

Breastfeeding can of course continue even when you're back at work by expressing and freezing milk or moving to a pattern of early morning and bedtime feeds only. If you get your body into this rhythm before going back to work there shouldn't be any need to express at work if that's not what you want. The National Childbirth Trust (www.nct.org.uk) has extensive online advice for mothers and employers on the practicalities of continuing breastfeeding when back at work.

MUM'S G-SPOT: Missing out on milestones

> I don't like not being able to pop in and play whenever I feel like it during the work day, and feel bad that I'm not seeing milestones and firsts (talking, walking ...)

Guilt Gripped

> I try not to get too upset about not seeing the 'firsts' and concentrate on the fact that I'll see the 'seconds'... she'll do everything several times anyway.

The first step, the first word, the first giggle could be easily be missed whether you're a working mother or not. And what about the unpleasant firsts you might have side-stepped by being a working mother? Poo in the bath, sicked-up solids, biting pre-school peer, hissy-fits and 'no' are just some of the delights you might be pleased to have missed. In fact, mum-of-two Teresa reflects on how, in hindsight, missing some of her children's early development would have been preferable to missing later stages:

> If I were to do it again, I would work full-time when the children were babies, then take my career break when

they were almost school-age and see them through their first two years of school. I am simply not a baby person and felt that being at home with them at this age was a thankless task, especially as they would not be able to remember our time together.

GETTING A GRIP ON CHILDCARE GUILT

MUM'S G-SPOT: Length of time in childcare

- ***Paula:*** My daughter being in nursery for a longer working day than my husband makes me feel guilty. She's there from 8.45 until 5.45 Monday to Friday.

- ***Karen:*** I feel that my son is in nursery too long and feel bad when I prioritize work over leaving to pick him up and so don't get him as early as I would like. I feel guilty that my two children are regularly the last ones in nursery to be picked up. It's OK in the summer when they're enjoying running about in the garden but when it's so dark and drizzly in the winter the guilt seems to double.

Guilt Gripped

- ***Paula:*** I work to keep a roof over our heads. How much guilt would there be if we didn't have a home?

- ***Imogen:*** I manage my guilt by remembering all the fun we have doing something together like dancing to a CD or racing down the alley. I think I'll always feel some guilt and I have to remind myself it's a balancing act and the alternative would have lots of disadvantages, too. I am helped by the fact that his nursery is excellent and I am really confident of his environment there.

- **Karen:** I've sorted out a work-from-home half-day so that I can spend more daylight time with the two beautiful little ones. I've made an arrangement with my mum that she picks up the children one night a week which means I can catch up on work if needed or, more often, indulge in an extra half-hour run to give me more sanity for the week ahead.

Feeling guilty is a personally owned emotion and a waste of effort. No one says 'great, she's feeling guilty'. Life's a compromise in so many ways but we really don't need to make it harder on ourselves. Think of the fabulous role model you are being by combining work with parenting.

MUM'S G-SPOT: Childcare that's not ideal

- **Hannah:** I feel guilty that I leave my daughter with carers who are not mothers.

- **Kathryn:** I feel guilty about leaving the children with someone else, as young children are meant to be with their mothers as Nature intended, and wondering is the childcare right? Are they being properly looked after?

Guilt Gripped

Is your guilt reasonable? Would you be happy with any form of childcare? If you can acknowledge that you would probably find fault with, and feel guilty about leaving your child with, Mother Teresa herself, then it's time to let this one go. If on the other hand your childcare really doesn't feel right – and that might only become apparent after you've been back at work for a bit – then do consider making a change. Have a look at the chapter which shows you how to fulfil the working mum's mantra *find childcare that fits your family*.

- **Julie:** I know that if I was at home full-time I wouldn't be happy. I only work three days which I think makes me feel better. I also changed from a day nursery to a nanny because I liked the idea of them being at home more, in a familiar environment.

- **Josephine:** I tell myself my children benefit from the environment they are in with other children and being stimulated in a way I may not have the patience for.

- **Kathryn:** I've arranged it so grandparents do the childcare wherever possible, as I know that their focus/attention is on the children. I think it's good for children to spend time with grandparents to form a strong relationship with them and I tell myself that other childcare situations may stimulate and socialize the children. I also recognize that having some time at work makes for more enthusiasm towards the children when we're together.

MUM'S G-SPOT: Using childcare when children are ill

- **Amanda:** I find it so difficult trying to work around my son being ill. If he cannot go to nursery, I often have to ask grandparents if they can look after him so I can go to work. My mother only ever seems to see Alexander when he is ill. It pains me to think about leaving Alexander when he is ill and needs his mummy.

- **Lu:** Having to take my baby to nursery even when I know she's not feeling 100 per cent well, and could do with a couple of days at home cuddling with Mummy, really tugs at my heart.

Guilt Gripped

- **Hazel:** There have been times my son has been ill and I've thought he would be better off staying with me but it would have been very complicated to have dropped things at work so I've taken him to nursery. I felt bad but what made me feel a little bit better is imagining some other reason that I couldn't look after him, like if I was seriously ill. I think we sometimes beat ourselves up not because we're leaving our kids *per se* but over what we're leaving them for.

- **Imogen:** My eldest child has been poorly since she was a baby with congenital problems. We've learned to live with it as a family and cope as well as we can. We have a nanny who feels like a part of the family so leaving my daughter with her, in our home, makes things much easier. If you have a child who seems prone to illness, having a nanny is probably the way to go to ease the guilty feeling if you have to work on your child's off days.

- **Lu:** I try and work from home on the days I feel she is not very well so that I can be called in any emergency and be there as soon as possible for her.

GETTING A GRIP ON DOMESTIC GUILT

This is a classic example of the 'damned if you do, damned if you don't' guilt thing. Talking to mums in general, just as many complain they feel guilty for *not* doing enough domestic chores (so they can spend more time with kids or doing something less boring than the housework instead) as for doing domestic stuff (therefore not doing something more interesting or playing with the kids). As mum-of-two Sasha says, 'I feel guilty if I don't feed my children good home-cooked food, but then feel just as guilty if I'm cooking when I could be playing with them.'

I say get the kids doing the cooking and the cleaning with you – though draw a line at chopping onions with your finest sabre or dragging your hoover upstairs, as my son likes to tell me he's capable of.

There's a load more on handling domestic guilt and getting on top of the housework in the next chapter: Go for 'Good Enough' at Home.

MUM'S G-SPOT: Not doing all the stuff that stay-at-home mums do

> I feel guilty about not being around after school, not being available for school trips and not being able to go to assembly every week. She is unable to have friends back after school; any reciprocation has to be done at weekends.

Guilt Gripped

- **Susanna:** My child understands why I am not around as much as I would like to be. I compensate by ensuring I drop him off in the mornings, go to the important assemblies and always go to school for birthday week. He has known nothing else and accepts I have to work.

- **Wendy:** I try to spend quality time with my daughter at the weekends, and do things she really likes to do. I also try to show her how much I love her with lots of cuddles when I'm with her.

- **Sara:** Sometimes I catch myself cherry-picking the good points about being a stay-at-home mum when I feel bad about going to work and not being able to do all the activities with my son that some of his friends do. Then I wake up and see all the things we CAN do because I work. Being at home all day would be awful for me and so that would have a knock-on effect on him.

GETTING A GRIP ON WORK GUILT

MUM'S G-SPOT: Not giving as much to my work as I used to

I feel guilty about not being able to give 100 per cent to my work – wanting to devote a little more of my life to work and the associated feelings of selfishness it brings.

Guilt Gripped

The most uplifting, to-the-point piece of guilt-gripping advice a mum has sent me has been this one:

I've decided that I give my employer great value for money and so I won't feel guilty about not being around at the odd time when I cannot be here (for ANY reason). If I need to have time off for kids, family, or – heaven forbid – myself, I've just decided to think 'you know what, no one ever said at the end of their life: I wish I had worked more.' So I just don't feel guilty at work and I do the important things that I need to. I have to accept the fact that my career will not move as fast as I would have wanted for quite some years to come. I try to get the most out of work by being proactive rather than just 'doing the day job' i.e. I am a mentor for more junior staff and organize thought-leadership groups and learning sessions.

GETTING A GRIP ON RELATIONSHIP GUILT

MUM'S G-SPOT: Not having the same relationship with my partner

I feel guilty about nagging my husband about everything. He will never understand truly what it's like to be a working mother, but when he suggested I give up work and 'did nothing' I bit his head off.

Guilt Gripped

Working mother or not, we all know things change in a relationship when we have kids, partly because we don't have enough time to think about our own needs, let alone another adult's. It takes two people not to make time for one another, and I say daddies everywhere can probably make more of an effort to care for the mothers of their children. As my husband said when our second child, Artemis, was born 'You look after her and I'll look after you,' which lasted a while (and that was nice) and then he thought I didn't need it any more. But we all need to feel cared for and appreciated, and if your man isn't doing it for you then you need to let him know. Probably the best thing, as I espouse when I'm coaching people on feedback skills in the workplace, is to wait until he does something praiseworthy and make him feel so good he does it again. Might sound patronizing but it works. One mum of three children had this advice about choosing what to focus your after-work energy on – and it isn't organizing playdates or cleaning the kitchen:

Happy mummies make for happy babies. No situation will ever be perfect. Mums have got to put themselves and their relationship with their husband first, as those are the two most important things you can give the baby: (1) a happy you (2) a loving and secure relationship. Making time to enjoy them is for your sake, not just theirs.

MUM'S G-SPOT: Relying on family when my child is ill

Because I work about 80 minutes' journey away from the nursery, if the children get ill during the day I either feel guilty they have to sit it out until I get back or guilty that I've got to ask my mother to break into her day and pick up the poorly one. She should get to see them when they're happy and playful, and she has her own life too! I feel guilty when I leave the boys when they are ill even if they are staying with my mum. I feel even worse putting them in nursery.

Guilt Gripped

My mum is great at reassuring me she doesn't mind and that we have it much harder than her generation. I always tell her how much I appreciate it and treat her to things to show I mean it. Hopefully her being there with the kids when they're ill means they'll forge an even closer bond. That's what I tell myself anyway. I talk to myself in a positive way reminding myself they are in good hands, probably with people who have more patience than me so they will have better care. If they are staying with my mum I already know how well they are being cared for.

GETTING A GRIP ON SELF-GUILT

Isn't it often the case that we think about ourselves last of all? Self-guilt is the guilt about not developing ourselves, not making time for our hobbies, to go to the gym, to see our friends, to chill out and nurture ourselves. Perhaps out of all the guilt in this chapter it's the most positive in that maybe its effect is to drive us towards finding greater space and time for ourselves. How to do just that and keep your relationships with friends, family and partner is the subject of the final working mum's mantra in the chapter called Do What It Takes to Thrive.

TOP 10 GUILT-GRIPPERS

Encompassing what you've read already and a little bit more, here are my top 10 guilt-gripping techniques.

1. **Accept that a certain level of guilt** is inevitable, especially if you're prone to excessively high standards. Remember you can't be all things to all men, babies or bosses and why would you want to be?

2. **Relabel 'guilt' as 'dissatisfaction'** or use another word instead. Sometimes it's not really guilt we're feeling so to call it so might unjustly intensify the feeling.

3. **Look for the silver lining** of the potentially guilt-inducing situation you're in. When you focus on the positives there's less room for the negatives and you promote a better feeling in the people around you, including your child.

4. **Expect guilty feelings to pass** and try to distract yourself if you catch yourself beginning to ruminate.

5. **Spend time with radiators, not drains.** Surround yourself with people who boost your self-esteem and don't reinforce guilt. Friendships can be the hardest of all relationships to end but if they consistently give you a bad feeling it's probably best to withdraw.

6. **Make balanced decisions using your head and your heart.** Then if guilt creeps in later you can recall your sound decision-making process.

7. **Have service level agreements with yourself.** These are expectations that you think are fair and achievable and you agree that guilt is undeserved if you are operating within those limits. For example, no guilt about not spending enough time with your child if you have done X, Y and Z with her this week.

8. **Be selective about who can 'make' you feel guilty.** Consider what drives other people's points of view and how that might be irrelevant to your situation. Do you really care what so-and-so from your postnatal class thinks? Do they really have your best interests at heart and do they know the full story of your life? Oh, and remember: no one can 'make' you feel anything.

9. **Remember the bigger picture** when you feel guilt in the moment. Guilt is usually a situational, in-the-moment kind of feeling but there's probably a bigger, positive reason why you've made the decision that's led you to this fleeting feeling of regret.

10. **Go for 'good enough' as a mantra for life** and watch 50 per cent of your guilt fly out the window. Give yourself a reality check by asking 'would my husband feel guilty about this?'

Exercise

Getting a Grip on Your Guilt

Like the mothers above, you too can get a grip on the guilt you might be feeling.

Divide a sheet of paper into three columns. In the first write down anything you feel guilty about. In the second write down how you could reframe or *think* differently about the situation to lessen your guilt. In the third write down any actions you could take to lessen your guilt or assuage it altogether. As one mum of three says: 'I think when you say something out loud like ''I feel guilty for working too much,'' ''not earning enough'' or ''putting my children in childcare'' it suddenly doesn't seem as bad as you thought.'

GUILT	NEW THINKING	ACTIONS
Feeling excited about being me again and not being at home all day with Harry.	It's good for me and Harry if I feel positive about going back to work; I'll enjoy spending time with him more when it's more precious.	Make a point of getting excited about going back to work and buying new clothes; book some KIT days in with new manager; agree return date; find singing group Harry and I can do on Mondays.
Leaving Harry for 10 hours a day in a nursery that I'm not sure about – girls all seemed too young.	They wouldn't be there if they weren't qualified; would I be happy even if they had 10 years' experience?	Ask to spend some time in the nursery with Harry to see what goes on before I go back to work; meet Harry's key worker and get to know her a bit.
Leaving work early and taking days off if Harry's ill when I've only just come back to work.	My boss is a working parent, he must know what it's like? Chris can take time off work too and it might not happen.	Let new boss know this is a concern and judge reaction now and see about possibilities to work from home; mention to Chris so he expects to share in the problem if Harry is ill.
Not making home-cooked food, relying on ready meals.	He's going to get good food at nursery and ready meals are much better than they used to be.	Make sure we all have fresh veggies every day at least; enjoy cooking a home-made meal at the weekend and once in the week – freeze leftovers for week after.

KEY IDEAS & ACTION POINTS
The mum's mantra for this chapter is 'Get a grip on guilt.'

- **Learn from others**: Look around and compare yourself to others if it helps. Take the words of advice from the mums in this chapter and try and live by the ideas that resonate with you.

- **Who's bothered?** Consider the possibility that you might be heaping guilt on yourself when the other people involved, particularly your child, are not concerned.

- **Make a plan**: Do the activity above to understand your G-spots and how you can avoid having them rubbed up the wrong way.

MUM'S MANTRA

6

Go for 'Good Enough' at Home

How to keep the domestic plates spinning

Happy mess is better than miserable tidiness.
TOM HODGKINSON, AUTHOR OF *THE IDLE PARENT*

I've never wanted to be 'good' at anything: 'brilliant' or 'awesome' definitely, but never 'good'. Well, it's kind of insulting, isn't it? Like if someone came to dinner and described your cooking as 'nice'. But since becoming a parent I've found a whole new respect for the word 'good', especially in relation to domesticity. Don't get me wrong, I still have Hyacinth Bouquet moments, but I try and direct those perfectionist tendencies into something more worthy than the towels and sheets in my airing cupboard. Like me, women I've coached say going for good enough on the domestic front has been liberating and (social) life-saving.

> *'Don't try to be Supermum. You need to change your behaviour and the expectations of your family as you really cannot do everything at home as well as work.'*

Living the 'good enough' mantra of this chapter means we have more space and time for the things we want to look back on and be proud of (because I for one realize I won't be including shots of a well-ordered airing cupboard in the home videos I make to reminisce over when I'm lined and losing it).

As BBC journalist Winifred Robinson says: 'What has made me a much happier mother is accepting that in trying to do it all I make myself tired and miserable and make my son and husband feel the same.' Clare, a mum who works full-time, says, 'I've given up running round constantly clearing clutter and getting rid of grime because I know it won't be long before it's messed up again. Any more than good enough is a waste of time and energy.'

WHY WE NEED TO GO FOR GOOD ENOUGH

Mary Gregory, an Oxford professor who's done a stack of research into employment and pay issues affecting working mothers, quipped in conversation with me that 'mothers in general are not a crowd of moaning minnies, but they do live close to permanent practical and emotional overload and cope magnificently.' She's absolutely right and I think for this reason we owe it to ourselves to make 'good enough' the golden goal at home. Too many of us expect, and do, more than we can reasonably cope with.

> *'My top tip is don't do any housework when on maternity leave so your husband doesn't get used to it being done.'*

Psychologist Chloe Bird did a study of the amount of domestic labour performed by 1,256 men and women and its impact on depression levels. Men reported doing 42 per cent of the housework and the women 68 per cent (which doesn't quite add up, of course, and according to other researchers who've studied housework habits, that's because men tend to over-report how much they do). Using clever statistical analyses Dr Bird determined the point at which people experience 'psychological distress' from inequity in the division of housework, and concluded that: 'inequity in the division of household labour has a greater impact on distress than does the amount of household labour. On average women are performing household labour beyond the point of maximum psychological benefit, whereas men are not.'

Remember the working mum's mantra #4: See Your Family as a Team. Housework needs to be shared and aspirations of perfection knocked on the head for the good of everyone, as *Guardian* journalist Lucy Cavendish alludes to:

> After the birth of my fourth child, I became so totally domesticated - cleaning and cooking cupcakes and breast-feeding all the time - that I even surprised myself. For some reason I felt that if I ran a tight ship - happy, clean children with clean fingernails, contented baby, happy husband who came home to a meal and fresh linen on the bed - everyone would notice and say: 'Isn't she amazing?' I soon snapped out of that. No one noticed, no one cared, everyone thought I'd lost my mind.

WHAT IS GOOD ENOUGH?

The good enough mindset is really about being comfortable with not doing something to the best of your ability but to a *sufficient* level. What is *good enough* or *sufficient* to you may be over the top or not enough to someone else. Several of the mums I spoke to said it doesn't come naturally to them, although Sarah says she's getting there:

> I hate the good enough mind set as I was fastidious about domestic chores before children. I think you have to eventually accept it otherwise you would go mad. I would much rather spend time with my daughter than clean, plus with a toddler everything in the house gets messy very quickly.

> 'I am happy to be good enough, I genuinely wish I was better but I was never that great before I had him! Domesticity is not my forte.'

I think there are two good ways to develop the 'good enough' habit. One is to draw a time boundary around a specific task, for instance, 15 minutes to give the kitchen a once over at the end of the day. When the oven timer beeps you walk away and revel in how good you are at being disciplined.

> '"Good enough" frees me up to have a life beyond being a working mother/wife, which has a knock-on benefit for my family because I am less resentful about the time I spend with/on them.'

Incidentally I've found through my coaching work that being disciplined in one aspect of life helps with other areas, too, which is good news if you're trying to stick to an exercise regime or save money.

The second approach is to imagine the domestic task in front of you done to perfection and then do it to, say, 70 per cent of that standard. Not easy to quantify, I know, although the mum who told me she only irons the front of things has clearly got it:

A perfectionist by nature, your 'go for good enough' saying only rings true because it has to. Now I'm back at work I think it's good enough to sometimes clean the bathroom with wipes rather than proper cleaning products, it's good enough to iron clothes on one side only and not to iron kiddies' clothes at all, and definitely good enough to cook a roast on a Sunday and then feast on the home-cooked leftovers until Tuesday!

> 'Good enough basically means making sure the to-do lists in my diary are adhered to and birthdays, etc. aren't forgotten. At the end of the day there will always be dusting to do.'

Another mum says the boundary thing resonates with her:

> I'm definitely a 'good enough' mum. I try to set time aside where the children know I am busy doing stuff (and let them 'help' if possible – my daughter is really good at putting her things away out of the dishwasher, pairing socks and setting the table). We have time where I am 100 per cent devoted to them, which makes borders clear.

Exercise

How You Can Live the Good Enough Mindset

Get a piece of paper and give it a nice determined heading such as 'HOW TO BE GOOD ENOUGH' and doodle round it to make it look like an attractive proposition.

Divide your paper into two columns: label the left column 'Too Much' and the right 'Good Enough'.

Under the left column make a list of the things that you do to a high, time-consuming standard on a regular basis. Don't judge or evaluate, just write down what comes to mind when you think of time-consuming domestic chores.

Now consider in what ways you could reduce the time spent thinking about and doing these activities. Scribble anything that comes to mind in the right column, again without judging. Write whatever you think of.

Finally, if there's any advice you've given yourself in the right-hand column that you think is really good, really worth following, write it on a pretty post-it note and stick it on your fridge until the habit's ingrained. Sixty-six days is the official average reported by psychologists as the time it takes to make a new habit.

A CLEANER OR A TAKEAWAY?

Good enough cleaning is about just that: cleanliness. Spot-lessness is way beyond good enough, as this mum says: 'Cleanliness matters more than tidiness, especially with a child. It doesn't matter to me any more that there is a mas-sive pile of toys, or washing to put away, as long as the floors and kitchen are clean.'

> *'I have tried not to tidy the kitchen or bedrooms straight away or tidy the lounge and playroom in an evening, but I find it impossible. I do think the "good enough" notion is great in theory and I wish it was in me to stick to this, but being tidy is my way of showing I can cope.'*

There's nothing wrong with a spotless home so long as you haven't paid the price in blood, sweat and tears either whilst you were doing it or when it all becomes spotty again. Pound sterling is the only price you want to pay for a clean home, preferably once a week by someone reliable and hardwork-ing. I used to think having a cleaner was an indulgence and now see it's an efficient way of managing family life. After two-and-a-half years I still sporadically text Annie to tell her she's wonderful.

Depending on location, a cleaner costs somewhere be-tween £6 and £12 an hour, which I defy any working fam-ily who has a weekly takeaway to say they can't afford. A number 11, a 35, a pilau rice and a garlic naan or never hav-ing to get into all the nooks and crannies or descale a show-er ever again? The choice is yours.

> *'I don't feel the need to have every toy put away once they are in bed now I am back at work. When I was at home full-time tidying everything away was my cue that it was adult time after spending all day with them.'*

The feel-good factor aside, the major benefit of having a cleaner is that less time is spent on cleaning overall. Knowing the toilets, basins, floor and whatever else *is* going to get done once a week means we're less inclined to be doing things every day to keep on top of it. I've found since having a cleaner I'm not tempted to clean a toothpaste-stained sink or give the living room a quick going over because I don't feel so responsible for it. In short, letting the cleaner clean takes a disproportionate amount of stress away – as Karen says:

I do very little cleaning now. I have a cleaner once a week for two-and-a-half hours and she mops floors, cleans bathrooms and vacuums throughout as well as a general flick dust. All that's left for me is the regular wipe-down in the kitchen after meals. I've stopped looking at the dust under the bed and the finger marks on the windows/mirrors. When they get too bad, I ask the cleaner to do an extra hour and they're sparkling again.

> *'As long as it's not dirty it's good enough. Mess and clutter are excusable.'*

The Value of a Cleaner

If you're in any doubt about the value of a cleaner, think about what an hour of your time is worth. Is it really better for you to clean when you could be relaxing in the bath, catching up with friends or playing pirates and building dens with your children?

One mum who works full-time shares this sentiment:

> I treated my maternity leave as a break, as a getting-to-know-my-child year and as time to spend with my baby. I did not prioritize housework, cooking or cleaning, as I knew I wanted to go back to work and would not have anything like that time again to enjoy my baby. Obviously I did do housework but I never took over all of it or assumed responsibility any more than I did whilst out at work. I tried to go without a cleaner for the first few months to save money but then I gave in and it was the best decision I made.

> 'The children and I have lots of fun on my days off. I generally do housework/getting children ready until about 9.30 on my days off from work, and then a little bit during quiet time (about an hour in the afternoon). The children and I can enjoy one another without the house looking a complete tip.'

Many women I've spoken to say the resistance to a cleaner comes from their partner who knows the cost of everything and the value of, well not quite nothing, but definitely not hired help. (Probably because you've been doing such a good job of keeping everything together.) One way to bring about a change in attitude could be to impress on him the difference it will make to *his* life in particular: a more relaxed home, a happier wife, less nagging (if he's not doing much then up the ante so a cleaner becomes more attractive) and more time for other things you'd all rather do. Sarah advises families to buy in as much help as they can afford:

Don't feel guilty about it – at the end of the day your relationship with your partner will be better as you will be less stressed and you will be able to spend more quality time with your children, which is much more important that maintaining a neat and tidy house.

This isn't the place to go into your joint relationship with money and how you organize your finances (for that I recommend *Sheconomics* by Professor Karen Pine and Simonne Gnessen), but suffice to say that if you want a cleaner, get one and have done.

> 'When I went back full-time I really didn't want to spend my time at the weekend cleaning. Now I am part-time I can't really justify it, but if I could afford it I would! Otherwise, don't try and do everything all the time, make a realistic to-do list and don't worry if you don't get it done.'

If a cleaner isn't an option I implore you to avoid running round like a headless chicken doing it when your baby's in bed. It doesn't harm little ones to see parents cleaning. In fact, unless you want your child to grow up thinking magic cleaning pixies take care of it, I suggest you thrust a pair of marigolds at them as soon as they're old enough not to eat them. Apart from anything else, children can find fun in just about anything we do with them; it's the spending time with us in playful mode that kids want, not necessarily an hour at *rumble tumble rotters* or *ya-ya yoga babes*.

All this said, there's one domestic chore that really should be left (if only to avoid heart-stopping moments) 'til little Tommy is in bed or, in fact, left altogether: the ironing.

ONLY OAPS SHOULD IRON TEA TOWELS

I'm probably doing many modern pensioners a disservice by suggesting they've got nothing better to do than iron tea towels, and for that I apologize, but surely they're only one of a handful of demographics who can justify it?

If you're still making time to iron tea towels, underpants (oh yes, there are women out there doing this) or bed linen, surely you must see that you can never again claim not to have enough time to yourself? In your defence you cry 'but they only take a minute and crisp bed linen does feel so much nicer', which is fine until you realize keeping up the ironing game only feeds other perfectionist tendencies. That's because habits are linked and one begets another – topple one bit of perfection and you're more likely to relax and let other things slide. And that's a good thing when you consider what you could be doing instead. As one mum jokes: 'The good news is I've stopped ironing about 50 per cent of what I used to, but I've become very anal about how wet washing is hung out to dry to minimize creases! Time saved here means more time for me.'

I never thought I'd be able to put 'extensive knowledge of the ironing habits of UK mothers' on my CV. But having asked a lot of women with young children about what they let slide when they went back to work, I now know quite a bit. Over 60 per cent of the mums I spoke to ranked ironing as the number-one thing they stopped or seriously reduced when they went back to work. Some are buying more clothes that look good without the hot metal treatment whilst others only iron the front of work clothes, use the tumble dryer more, embrace the crumpled look or get someone else to do it. Like Karen: 'No more ironing kids' clothes unless it's a party, never bedclothes, and hubby's shirts get left until last every week which means he inevitably gets frustrated and irons his own. Result!'

Let's Salute Crumpled Clothes

When Artemis was born and my multi-tasking spiralled beyond hysterical (folding freshly tumbled towels behind the wheel at traffic lights on my way back from the launderette) my husband decided the least he could do was take over the ironing whilst watching Saturday's C4 racing. I believe this is the only multi-tasking he's ever done, and from him I've learned a lot about the benefits of doing one thing at a time. Nick continues to iron, although never tea towels, bed linen or children's clothes, and I continue to salute parents of children in crumpled clothes. I've become a sort of inverse domestic goddess, mentally praising mums who haven't bothered to iron (lest vocal praise embarrass or be taken the wrong way) thinking they obviously have – and indeed do – better things with their time. It's these women we should make a beeline for at playgroups for interesting conversation! As Emma says: *Does anyone say on their deathbed that they wish they had done more ironing?*

> '*DELEGATE as many household chores as you can (even to children, e.g. get them to hang up their own coats, put dirty clothes in the laundry basket, set the table, return their plates to the kitchen). All of this instantly gives you more time for the important things. And for God's sake don't iron bedding! Fold it all straight after washing/drying and it will look fine – life's too short!*'

Other mums are clearly applying the 'life's too short' logic to laundering clothes, too:

I've got better things to do with my evenings than listen out for the end of the wash cycle, so I keep all the washing to one or two nights a week and only change *the beds once a fortnight. I used to do it every week but with three sets of bedding it's too much to spend every Friday night doing three or four extra loads on top of clothes washes.*

TV's popular cleaning duo Kim and Aggie could probably wow us with sweat secretion and bed bug statistics, but I can live with the same sheets for 13 nights to reduce the laundry burden. Can you? Other mums say they sponge light marks on their children's clothes and live with milk-stained cardigan shoulders to reduce the wash pile. If you're shuddering at the thought of looking like you're going for a bit part in *Oliver!*, worry not, I'm just suggesting you question whether stuff needs the wash bin at the end of the day rather than chucking it there by default.

FEEDING THE FAMILY

From stains and soap suds to shopping and sustenance, what's your take on 'good enough' food for your family? Given the brilliant work of Jamie Oliver with UK school dinners and Hugh Fearnley-Whittingstall's fight to put an end to battery-farmed chickens and wasted fish, we're all a lot more conscious of what's going in our mouths these days. I even heard a story on the news about Ofsted inspectors finding some nurseries were giving their children *too much fruit*. Yes, too much fruit. It's everything in moderation you know, not just salt and sugar!

Food and feeding time can be a source of stress whether parents work or not, but it needn't be. Online shopping, a moderate approach to home-cooked versus shop-bought meals and everyone eating the same are three ways to take some of the sting out of mealtimes.

'When you think of how long it would take to get there, do it yourself with a grumpy/tired child, push a heavy trolley around, load the car, get home and unpack, multiplied by your hourly wage, online shopping is priceless no matter the cost. Especially as your child gets older and food shopping is no longer a novelty fun activity.'

Shop Online and Save Your Life

Before I did online shopping I looked forward to going to the supermarket for 'me time'. Then I woke up to myself and got a life along with an awful lot of carrots (8 kg as opposed to the '8' I thought I'd ordered, which gave the nursery mums a good laugh when I shared the bounty next day). For less than a bottle of cut-price Chardonnay super-markets will pick, pack and deliver your groceries within an hour window any day of the week you choose. Is it only me who gets excited about that? No worrying about whether you can fit a shop in between feeds or how much negotia-tion you'll have to do with a toddler to get round and out in relative peace. Oh yes, online shopping is a *must* especially as you can do it at work when no one's watching *and* keep an eye on how much you're spending. This mum shares my fervour:

I do it at lunchtime and because you can save your list for future shops I can go back to old orders and think, 'Ooh yes, that's what we'll eat this week.' I've got over them sending darker apples than I would pick and missing out reduced bargains if it means I can read the paper or stay in bed longer on a Saturday morning.

Home-cooking and Oh-so-wonderful Ready Meals

Reduced bargains, there's a talking point. Being a northerner I get a *lot* of satisfaction from filling up my overflow garage freezer with supermarket's half-price 'better than a Michelin-starred gastro pub' ready meals. I love the double saving of time and cash, though given half the chance I'd happily while away a couple of hours batch cooking every weekend if I were allowed to do it on my own save for Vernon Kaye/Jonathan Ross/Evan Davies for radio company. Instead I regularly feed my family other people's cooking and, so long as there's a big heap of brightly coloured veg alongside a ready lasagne, coq au vin or fish pie, that's fine by me.

What I do think is really important are families eating together as much as possible. When I say 'eating together' I mean eating the same thing as much as at the same time. I'm convinced that fussy eaters are made by parents giving their kids both too much and not enough choice in what they eat.

What do I mean? Somehow in the UK we've got to thinking that kids only like a certain subset of food or that it's right for us to offer only a limited range to them. Whilst I don't have a research paper to back me up I'm pretty confident there are a lot of kids out there who only know about fish fingers, pasta, chicken nuggets, sausages, pasta, sandwiches, jacket potato, pizza and did I say pasta? I'm not criticizing these things, I eat them and so do my kids. What I'm saying is that there's so much more besides, and the average kid in Britain isn't tasting any of it. That's what I mean about not enough choice.

Feed Your Children the Food You Like to Eat

At the same time, many parents give too much choice to their very young children when they let them decide what to eat. Knowing only a limited range, kids ask for the same stuff time and again. My kids would never have asked for coq au vin, tofu bean burgers or ratatouille (and they still don't but they bloody well eat it or go hungry) if I hadn't introduced them to it. And so it is they eat lots of different things, and it's a pleasure to share a meal when they let us talk and keep the floor clean. Which, admittedly, very rarely happens unless they are falling asleep on their plates.

I say all this out of concern for the working mums who are stressing themselves out about what to feed their families, like this Mumsnetter:

> I've just bought a new toddler recipe book to give me inspiration for inclusive family meals and am balking at the meal planner. I thought it was just an Annabel Karmel phenomenon that one is meant to spend all day every day shopping for fresh ingredients and cooking up gourmet delights, but this book (which is written by dieticians and has much more achievable recipes in general) still has loads of recipes which can take an hour or more to prepare, and with such a wide variety of ingredients over the week. Am I alone in feeling overwhelmed by the prospect of trying to ensure my toddler has a snowball's chance of eating a properly balanced diet?

Of course she's not alone and my heart goes out to her for being suckered into thinking she has to make 'toddler' meals. As one mum said to me:

> The cuteness soon went out of cooking special separate meals for our daughter when I went back to

work and although we often don't eat together she eats for her dinner the next night what we had the night before.

If you're into cookbooks, you'll love the ease and speed of recipes in Jamie Oliver's *30-Minute Meals*. The man himself gave the following advice on a live Mumsnet webchat:

I've worked in the last eight years with many families and mothers that are tearing their hair out trying to cater for everyone's individual tastes. I've witnessed mothers cooking five different meals for their kids and husbands – love will drive you to deliver that. At some point you have to stop, rethink, and find enough things that they have in common and feed them one big tasty meal. You've got to be a bit more strict about it. You may have tears and a bit of playing up for a day or two, or a week, but ultimately if they are hungry, they will eat.

Midweek Meal with Mini-me

It's tough that many families can't eat together because of the way they need to balance childcare drop-offs and pick-ups (one parent going in early whilst the other works late) or long commutes. My answer is a campaign I'm yet to start to get employers to encourage their staff to get home on a Wednesday to eat dinner as a family. Turning a blind ear to the uproar from singletons or those without kids, I'm stating here and now that families are an important part of society and it's our kids who'll be paying the childless couples' pensions, so let's call it payback.

'I'm less adventurous in the kitchen mid-week, leaving my culinary experiments to the weekends when it's much more appreciated by a relaxed hubby and even a few chums we might have invited over, too.'

If you can find a way to meet at mealtimes then do it, it's good on all sorts of levels, not just for keeping faddy eating at bay. Sam's married to a farmer and they usually have breakfast together or find another way to have time every day as a family: 'If my husband is not lambing or in the middle of harvest, he'll usually come in for a cup of tea at bathtime so we can be together and talk about our day.'

Friends and Food

I don't know about you but I haven't had our wedding list dinner service and posh cutlery out much since having kids. I haven't cooked a three-course meal from scratch since they were born, either. Having friends over now usually means cooking in the presence of our pals, kids setting the table with the everyday crockery and cutlery and a bought pudding with custard from a can served in a Pyrex jug. And you know what, I'm sure I'm better company these days. Proper friends wouldn't give a damn whether you served cheese sandwiches on paper plates or cheese soufflés in Royal Doulton ramekins. If they're working parents themselves they're probably relieved you didn't suggest meeting up at *Pizza Express*, and as Carrie says, they haven't noticed the state of your house:

People rarely visit your house to inspect how clean and tidy it is – generally they're there to spend time with you and your family. They don't care if your skirting boards are dusty — well, I don't when I go to see my friends.

A Word on Kids' Parties

Whilst not something you'll be thinking about day to day – unless you are in fact a children's entertainer, in which case you might want to skip this bit – kids' parties can be a pain in the posterior for working parents, especially if the synthetic party packages of the modern era grate with you. This email party invitation from a dear friend made my heart sing – and not least because it frees us all from the kids' party arms race:

> Dear all
>
> We are having a birthday party for Farrah next Saturday 24th July from 2.30 p.m. to 4 p.m. at Charles Hall, St Merton.
>
> We were going to do a casual drop-in-at-the-park thing, but given the risk of rain (she was born in the middle of a massive thunderstorm, after all), we have, at the very last minute, decided to book this.
>
> I can't promise bouncy castles, musicians or anything exciting to two-/three-year-olds, but there are swings there and a big field to run around, plus the hall itself to take cover in, play with toys, eat cake, etc.
>
> As it's a mid-afternoon thing, I don't think we will be doing full catering, but some cakes, dips, drinks, etc. will be on offer. May even be able to stretch to a game of pass the parcel!
>
> Please let me know if you think you can make it.
>
> Grace x

KEY IDEAS & ACTION POINTS

The working mum's mantra for this chapter is 'Go for "good enough" at home.'

This means putting domesticity in perspective and prioritizing the stuff that really matters. For sure there'll be times when you have the energy and inclination to make your kitchen pristine or the desire to organize the most amazing birthday party, but the key to staying sane is not to expect these things from yourself as standard.

Instead, here's a summary of what real working parents do – or ditch – on a regular basis to make their lives easier. Tape these to your fridge and live them:

1. **DO hire a cleaner** if you can: 'A cleaner makes the single biggest difference to my working week. She's a luxury and I'd rather not eat than forgo her!'

   DITCH trying to maintain the peak perfection achieved by the cleaner. Let your eyes feast for a moment on how wonderful the place looks then let it go until the same time next week.

2. **DO rein in domestic chores** by prioritizing what's really important to you. 'A year on from returning to work from my second period of maternity leave I have realized that there aren't enough hours in the week to work, spend quality time with the kids, keep the house clean and cook gourmet meals every night. I have to work and I have to spend quality time with the kids. Those two things are a given. The other stuff is just fluff.'

   DITCH impossibly high standards by ploughing your time into the things you want to look back on with pride, i.e.

your kids, your relationships, personal achievements. If it wouldn't feature in family videos, don't bother with it!

3. **DO share the domestic workload** as per mum's mantra #3: See Your Family as a Team. 'My husband and I split the chores and know our specific ones so we don't argue about the kitchen being a mess and so on. He has Saturday morning duties when I have a leisurely shower and relax.'

   DITCH interfering or redoing things if they're not done the way you'd have done it – a meal on the table is a meal on the table; an ironed shirt is an ironed shirt.

4. **DO put a time limit on how long you'll give to a task** and look for shortcuts: 'I used to do certain things by hand but now everything goes in the dishwasher so I can scoot upstairs for bedtime stories.' Washing up is only acceptable if it's code for staring out the window and getting some peace and quiet.

   DITCH running round like a headless chicken competing with yourself to squeeze more into less time. Multi-tasking can go too far, as per my laundry-folding at the traffic lights.

5. **DO minimize mess in the first place**. 'I get the kids dressed upstairs to keep the mess up there, eat outside in the summer to avoid getting the kitchen floor messy, keep toys in one room to avoid them overspilling to every room in the house.'

   DITCH constant clearing up – we only get frazzled and frustrated at how quickly it needs doing again.

6. **DO get the kids involved**. 'My two-year-old loves "helping" me and will quite happily wipe the walls or "dust" for me, while my four-year-old brings his plates to the dishwasher and puts his clothes in the laundry bin.'

DITCH thinking quality time with your child equals an organized activity. Kids can find fun in what you see as domestic drudge so long as you're playful and focused on them.

7. **DO iron absolute essentials** such as work clothes where impressions count: 'I purchase things that don't need ironing, haven't done any of the kids' stuff in ages and only do the front of shirts.'

   DITCH ironing kids' T-shirts, tea towels and bed linen.

8. **DO online shopping** and reclaim an hour for yourself midweek or at the weekend: 'There's no risk of my husband getting it wrong when he does online shopping as I can log in and double-check it!'

   DITCH walking supermarket aisles at the weekend and thinking it is a treat. You are worth more.

9. **DO make one meal for the family** and eat together as much as you can: 'It's a no-brainer, why waste time cooking two things when one will do? The biggest compliment a non-mummy friend once gave me was that our two-year-old son could come for lunch any time.'

   DITCH feeling guilty about not cooking from scratch every night.

10. **DO make friends a priority** and keep having them over for food and merriment because friendship is invaluable, as every parent knows: 'I so can't be doing with the whole big, over-the-top thing. I want to see my friends and they want to see us so we take it in turns and usually eat something shop-bought.'

    DITCH thinking your house has to be tidy and the food gourmet-standard before you have pals round to play.

Prepare for a Smooth Return

Your step-by-step countdown plan to making back-to-work a breeze

Proper preparation produces performance.
ANONYMOUS

N o one likes a doom-mongering know-it-all, but who-ever spouted 'she who fails to prepare, prepares to fail' was onto something. Along with the words *cleaner* and *not guilty*, 'get organized' features heavily in the vocabulary of working mums, and so the mantra for this chapter is *prepare for a smooth return*.

In this chapter you'll get a complete picture of what you can do to make the transition back to work as easy and smooth as possible. Written in a timeline format, you can dip in and out as R-day draws nearer, and tick off tasks for that week or day. But more than a series of to-do lists, I hope this chapter will breed confidence and optimism about the next stage of your working life, be that returning to the job you did before children or starting afresh.

WHAT NOT TO THINK ABOUT BEFORE BABY IS BORN

I detest shop windows stuffed with back-to-school uniform displays before the summer holidays as much as I detest Christmas advertising in September. Why? Because it spoils the time we're currently trying to enjoy. Prematurity has never been a good thing. So given this, I'm the last person who wants to spoil your maternity leave by suggesting there are a whole heap of things you should be doing to prepare for going back to work before your darling even arrives.

However, there *is* one thing lots of mums-to-be do before baby, and that's look into childcare options. I'm being deliberately vague by saying 'look into' as I don't want to freak you out with tales of mums who book nurseries as soon as they feel the baby kick for the first time. So much can change between getting pregnant and the time you actually go back to work that unless it makes you feel so much better organizing care this early then I wouldn't advise doing it. For the sake of keeping things flowing smoothly for everyone I think pregnancy test kits should be plastered with 'Please don't book childcare until one month before you go back to work' labels in the same way McDonalds used to display 'Please purchase food before finding a table' signage.

'LUCKY' CHILDCARE

Things have a way of working themselves out for the best if you believe they will. That's not airy-fairy nonsense to make you feel better if you haven't got childcare and you're going back next month. Psychologist and author of *The Luck Factor* Professor Richard Wiseman has shown that, to a large extent, people really do create their own luck. Increasing your good fortune according to Wiseman – whether that be finding the perfect nanny or securing a satisfying job close to home that also fits around school hours – boils down to four key principles:

1. **Pay more attention to chance opportunities and act on them.**

2. **Listen to your intuition.**

3. **Create self-fulfilling prophecies by having positive expectations.**

4. **Adopt a resilient attitude that transforms 'bad luck' into good.**

All this said, where there's great organization there's no need to rely on luck.

ADVANCED PLANNING

People often ask me how I keep myself organized. The best answer I can give is my paper week-to-view diary. I use my diary as a place to write personal and professional to-do lists for the week ahead, not appointments. The great thing about using a diary to store to-do lists is you can make a note of something for four or 40 weeks ahead and know that you'll remember it because it's in this one place. Taking things out of your head and putting them onto paper is one of the greatest tips I can give to any practically or emotionally overloaded person. I recommend trying this technique in the run-up to returning to work to help you plan what needs to be done and when.

> *I kept in touch with work throughout my leave and went in for celebratory drinks and some events when I could manage it.*

I've divided this next section under five headings to cover the things you'll want to have organized:

- three to six months before you return

- the month before

- the week before

- the day before

- the day itself.

Each section has sub-sections covering professional, personal, childcare and domestic concerns.

THREE TO SIX MONTHS BEFORE YOU RETURN

Professional

- **Legalities:** As you read in the Mantra #2 chapter, you are legally required to: 1) tell your employer of your child's birth if he comes before your maternity leave starts or if you return within six months of his birth and 2) put it in writing (at least eight weeks beforehand) if you plan to return to work before the end of your statutory entitlement of 52 weeks.

- **Return date**: If you didn't agree your return date before maternity leave or if you are looking for a new job, my advice is to set this date (or the date by which you want to have secured a new role) between three and six months before you want to start. Carrie: 'I always knew when I was going back. I think that helped. I've had friends who didn't have a set date and they never felt ready to return.'

- **KIT days:** The mums in the Mantra #2 chapter were adamant that keeping in touch with work really does make for an easier transition. Now is a good time to pick up the phone to arrange dropping in for a chat or organizing to join an away day, team meeting or a one-to-one with your boss to talk about your return. Jenny: 'I went into work for a couple of days (paid 'Keeping in Touch' days) – once for an away day and once for some training. It was good to see colleagues again and get back into work mode.'

- **Ideal scenario:** Recall your thoughts from the first two chapters about your ideal work scenario and asking for it. Make sure you cover these ideas in your back-to-work conversations.

'I caught up with all my work colleagues via email for the office gossip and how things were during the whole of maternity leave. Visited the office once with little one and once on my own about six weeks before my return date.'

Personal

Many women I've spoken to talk about being ready to claw back some time for themselves at this point. Perhaps you're ready to resume a hobby, get back into the gym or go out with friends in the evening. Of course, you may never have given these things up in the first place! Helena says 'I used to go to a running club before my son was born and by the time he was six months old I was more than ready to get back into it. Before then I was too tired in the evenings to contemplate it, but once he was sleeping through it was easier to find the energy and the will.'

Childcare

Now's the time to start looking into **childcare options**, which means considering the benefits and drawbacks of each and going to speak to would-be carers. Remember Mantra #4: Find Childcare that Fits Your Family. What might be the best thing since sliced bread according to one mum may be unsuitable for you – trust your intuition and keep an open mind.

- **Talk to local working mums** about the childcare they use. Ask why they like it and anything they'd change if they could so that you get a rounded picture.

- **Ofsted reports** (www.ofsted.gov.uk) may give you extra peace of mind about the care you are considering for your child. Read them before going to visit so you can pick up on any points of concern. For example, a nursery or child-minder may have been marked down for something that they have since rectified.

- **Visit at least three** of each type of care setting you are considering (i.e. three nurseries and/or childminders) in quick succession so you can make fresh comparisons. Use the list of questions from the Mantra #4 chapter and the additional ones you devised from the exercise 'Your Personalized Question List'.

- **Shortlist** the places you like the most and arrange to go back for a second visit if you want to, perhaps with a friend or partner for a second opinion.

- **Ask your friends or other local mums** for their opinions on the providers.

- **Arrange a schedule of settling-in sessions** for the month before you go back to work so you feel organized and can plan any Keep In Touch visits with work or other appointments. 'Make sure you are really happy with the childcare arrangements as it is so much easier to go back to work knowing your child is safe and happy. Allow plenty of settling-in time so you both get used to it.'

Domestic Duties

It's never too early to start adopting the 'go for good enough' mindset, so why not see your challenge at this point as starting to do things in a less than perfect way? Psychologists have shown that it's easier to *do* something than *not do* something (for example if I asked you not to think of pink elephants, guess what start dancing round your head?) so instead of deliberately trying to do less house work it's easier to do more of something else instead. That way you haven't got the time to be bothered about cleaning the cooker or dusting under the beds. What that something could be is up to you.

THE MONTH BEFORE YOU RETURN
Professional

- **Plan what you would like to talk about with your boss** before returning to work, including the suggestions below. Remember Mantra #2: Stay in Touch and Ask for What You Want. Make a few notes to act as a prompt at the meeting:
  - induction/handover plan
  - what your team has been doing recently
  - your role and objectives for the next six months
  - expectations around what you will achieve in your first month
  - support available to help you settle back in
  - expectations about flexible working and work hours
  - dates and times for weekly one-to-ones
  - a date and time for a longer review at the end of your first month.

- **Meet with your boss** and any other personnel who are key to your smooth transition. This might include some of your direct reports and your maternity leave cover, if applicable. It's *your* return to work so the more proactive you can be the better you'll feel – if you'd like to set a more relaxed tone suggest a lunch meeting somewhere you feel comfortable.

- **Consider KIT days** to re-familiarize yourself with your work environment and colleagues, as Tasha did: 'I made full use of the Keeping In Touch days and, during the month leading up to my return, I worked a day a week. I spent the time familiarizing myself with the latest projects/issues and going through all the emails I had received over the course of the year. I was also able to try out my newly agreed working hours (which take account of the school day in relation to my eldest child). It was a financial boost as by that time I was not earning maternity pay. I also did all my team's annual appraisals during this time, which meant I was well versed in their work and priorities when I started back properly.'

- **Phone a workmate** for a catch-up if you haven't been in touch during your leave. If you're starting somewhere new and you have the name and number of any of your colleagues drop them a line and organize a coffee before you start. It's this informal chat and getting to know someone personally that can grease the wheels at work.

- **Meet your 'parenting buddy'** if your organization runs such a scheme. Forward-thinking organizations are providing tools like this to make the comeback from maternity leave easier.

> *'I did a lot of project planning, lists of materials, etc. so when it came to the crunch a lot of my work thinking had already been done before I was officially back.'*

Personal

- **Clothes**: Be ruthless with your working wardrobe and pack anything that doesn't induce feelings of fabulousness off to the charity shop. A post-baby body and a fresh professional start are the ultimate reasons to see an image consultant *and* go shopping. Make shopping sprees focused and fruitful by having a list of key pieces, shoes and accessories you'll need.

- **Friends**: You might see less of them for a while when you're first finding your working feet, so enjoy your pals whilst you can. As Clare recalls: 'I met up with as many playdate friends as possible as I knew that this would be difficult when I went back to work. It helped with the change in focus.'

  You might be interested to know that in 2005 Australian researchers reported that keeping up with friends rather than family is also the key to a longer life. Researchers asked 1,500 over-70s about level of contact with children, relatives and friends, and monitored the results over a 10-year period. They found that close contact with children and other relatives had little impact on survival rates, but a strong network of friends and confidantes significantly improved longevity. Your friends' support could be just the ticket for helping you feel good about adjusting to life as a working parent, especially if they are working parents, too. Do remember to tell them you're going back to work, unlike Jennifer who didn't so had to spend lunchtimes and evenings calling people back to turn down playdates when she'd really rather have collapsed in a heap.

- **Well Woman appointments**: Get up to date with cervical smears, dental check-ups, eye tests, asthma clinic, hair cutting and colouring (yes, that's definitely Well Woman territory) and anything else that requires a weekday appointment. Helen: 'I had my hair cut and the grey dyed away. I went to see a personal shopper to get some new clothes I felt good in and professional after 12 months of casual dressing.'

Childcare

Many of the mums I surveyed mentioned the importance of settling their children into daycare arrangements well in advance. This is great advice for several reasons, and nearly every mum I spoke to said they really enjoyed the freedom to play, have fun, do what they want to do minus kiddie-winks in that final pre-work week. I remember literally skipping away in my running kit with A-Ha's 'The Sun Always Shines on TV' (there's no accounting for taste) blasting from my iPod when I left my son for two hours at the childminder's the first time. There's no shame in it, we all need personal space and time to think. We cannot be bountiful and giving if we don't take care of ourselves. In contrast to my story, a friend tells the tale of walking away from her son's nursery in a flood of tears the week before she was due back at work – not because she'd left him, but because she hadn't. They'd turned him away because of his heavy cold and my friend was distraught about missing out on the relaxed me time she'd been looking forward to.

- **Mums on starting childcare**: If you are able, arrange to start your child's transition into his or her daycare setting a month before you return. 'Try to sort out the arrangements as early as possible in order to get used to the change for all of you. Have a trial month before going back so you can iron out any problems whilst you are still away from work. I got a nanny to start about a month before I returned to work so I knew she would be OK and know what to do when I wasn't there, which gave me some peace of mind.'

- **Breastfeeding**: 'If you're breastfeeding, introduce bottle-feeding well in advance of your return to work – my child refused to bottle-feed and it almost scuppered my return to work (and caused us both a lot of anxiety).' The National Childbirth Trust (www.nct.org.uk) has detailed information about how to continue breastfeeding when back at work.

- **Contingency plans**: Children have a habit of having a lot of sniffles and minor ailments in their first year, but not necessarily to such an extent that you feel you need to be at home with them (even though the nursery or child-minder has sent them home). To avoid this causing you to take a lot of leave from work it's worth sounding out friends and family now about whether they would be able to help you when your little one is ill. Two mums on what they'd do, with hindsight:

I would collect more childminding contacts, as many as possible, even if just someone else's mum who needs a bit of extra money now and again. I would meet and informally interview all possible contacts as there wouldn't be time to do it once I'd started work. I would get these contacts to evening babysit a couple of times so that if I needed someone to look after my child in an emergency (e.g. ill childminder), they'd know where the house was and my son would have met them before.

I would have planned back-up childcare better. I hadn't realized quite how many illnesses my eldest son would pick up in the first few months after I returned to work and which blew my original childcare plans apart.

Domestic Duties

- **Rebalance the roles at home** by chatting to your partner and any older children or family who live with you about how you will all share the load when you are not at home full-time. Remember Mantra #3: – See Your Family as a Team. 'Be a little less efficient, because I believe my husband takes advantage of the fact that everything runs fairly ship-shape, and if I were a bit more dizzy I'd get more help.'

- **Start the rebalanced routine and responsibilities** a fortnight before you are back at work to iron out any niggles (but not kids' clothes or bed linen, remember!).

- **Meals planned** for the first few weeks after you're back is a good idea, but only if meal-planning is your responsibility. If meals are for your partner to think about, let him do it in his own way and own time.

- **Get that cleaner** that nearly every mum I surveyed on domesticity suggested we should. As one friend who's had her eyes opened to paid help now she lives in the US said to me: 'Jessica, never feel guilty about paid help. It's not a luxury to pay for help that makes daily life happen when you're working. Women with family nearby don't feel guilty about accepting grandparents' help and neither should you just because you pay for it.'

THE WEEK BEFORE YOU RETURN

All systems go, firing on all cylinders and time to settle into your new working groove minus the actually working bit. Do the morning routine as you would then have a cup of tea, chill out and do what you fancy before kicking into the evening routine as it'll happen next week.

Professional

In that space between the morning and evening routine you might want to do something work-related (assuming your child is in childcare) to help ease your mind back into it. The working mum's Mantra #2 was Keep in Touch and Ask for What You Want, and if you did the exercise 'Easing Yourself Back into Work' at the end of that chapter you might find it helpful to revisit your answers. If you didn't, spend a few minutes completing it now.

Personal

- **Confident self-talk**: Samantha: 'When I felt a bit "wobbly" about whether I'd still be able to do the job, I gave myself a good talking-to. If I could do it before there's no reason I couldn't now.'
  Hayley: 'I had a good chat with myself about not feeling bad about going to work. It is a good thing for me and for my family but I knew there would be days when my daughter would not want me to go. Having my calm voice of reason in my head on days when I wasn't feeling calm and reasonable helped so much.'

- **Remember why you're going back** and focus on these reasons to keep you looking forward to your return as one mum wishes she'd done: 'Although I cried for about a week before returning to work and felt as if it was being forced upon me by society I wouldn't change it now for anything. I love the balance of working three days a week.'

- **Treat yourself** in some sensational or small way. Although that haircare ad where she flicks her locks and says something about being worth it is a bit naff, the sentiment is great. Becoming a mother is a major life transition filled with giving; it's time to reclaim yourself by signalling to the world and yourself that you are indeed worth it. Go crazy and book yourself into a spa retreat.

Childcare

- **Do the routine** as it will be next week, for your child's benefit as much as yours. Our children pick up on our cues so if we can be calm and relaxed getting them ready, taking them to their carer and picking them up then it will have a good impact on them. 'I eased my daughter into nursery over a month before I went back to try and ensure she was settled before she did full days. I also did a dry run of the morning and evening routines and set up my home office too as I was working primarily from home.'

- **Organize doing the drop-offs and pick-ups** and mark them in you and your partner's diary for the first couple of weeks until it becomes routine.

- **Have fun, play** and enjoy being with your children in a relaxed, unplanned way to contrast with the organization it seems you're doing in every other sphere of life.

Domestic Duties

- **Online shopping**: book a delivery for the day before you go back.

- **House admin**: Get on top of paperwork and devise systems to make sure you stay on top. Chapter 5 of *Time Management for Manic Mums* by Allison Mitchell is brilliant for this.

- **Social life**: Buy cards, presents, costumes and anything else for any celebrations happening within your first working month. Wrap, label and organize things as much as possible now.

- **Laundry**: Get the washing and ironing up to date and in particular put yourself first and make sure any clothes you'll want to wear in your first week are clean and pressed.

THE DAY BEFORE YOU'RE BACK

Make today a day of keeping things calm, easy and without adventure so you feel rested and ready for tomorrow. If you're a spontaneous sort of woman who likes to pack a lot into her life rein in any ideas of redecorating your child's room or visiting that designer factory outlet 50 miles from home. In a word, chillax.

Professional

If there's something you want to do to get back into your professional mindset like reading a trade journal or going through any papers work has sent you, do it at your leisure. Otherwise everything else can surely wait until tomorrow. 'I took some time to open up my world by reading newspapers and watching the news, listening to politics. I felt this prepared me for some adult conversations and would give me something to discuss.'

Personal

- **Fun**: Plan to do something enjoyable such as spending time with people who make you feel good. Cream tea and a chat, anyone?

- **Outfit**: Decide what you're going to wear tomorrow and keep it in your wardrobe until the morning. Sticky fingers and sicky stains should not go with you tomorrow.

- **Travel**: Check travel pass is in handbag and/or enough petrol's in the car.

- **Kit**: Pack your bag (your work one, of course – this is no time to be filling a suitcase and running away from home).

Childcare

- **Routine**: Do the morning routine as you will need to do it tomorrow.

- **Day bag**: If your child is being cared for outside your home get their clothes ready and their bag packed for the morning. Better still, get your partner to take responsibility for your children and this. If you do delegate, remember to describe the outcome you are looking for and not the precise way to do it – your husband is not a monkey, let him think for himself.

- **Joy**: Enjoy your children and keep maudlin thoughts in check by focusing on the here and now. For certain your children are more beautiful, wonderful and happy-making than sliced bread but getting soppy will only make tomorrow harder. Stay away from the baby album!

- **Positivity**: Reread the guilt-grippers of the mums in chapter five and let any G-spot rubbing be of a very different kind tonight.

- **Check childcare**: Call your childcare provider to make sure they are expecting you tomorrow.

Domestic Duties

There's only one thing to do today on the domestic front (apart from all the usual gubbins) and that's to take delivery of your online grocery shop. Take a smug look at your fridge-freezer and rejoice that you have the week ahead's meals sorted.

YOUR FIRST DAY BACK

Professional

Aim to get out of first gear and up to second or third by the end of the day, and remember to go into neutral at home time. What do I mean? Go easy on yourself; today's not the day for proving your worth.

- **Access the building** and make sure you're up and running with any necessary equipment: office, desk, PC, mobile, log-in details, security card, parking space?

- **Smile, say hello** and take an interest in as many people as you can. Jobs are made or broken by relationships.

- If not in a new job, **glance at emails** that have accumulated in your absence. Select all and delete.

- Start working through your **induction plan**.

- **Go out at lunchtime** if only to flake on the nearest park bench to recover from possible information overload – particularly relevant if you're in a new job.

- **Leave on time** with head held high like an assertive male business-owner would. You need to start as you mean to go on; you have to respect your boundaries if others are to follow.

Personal

- Make it your mission to **enjoy commuting**. This is free headspace time that not even public transport overcrowding can spoil. Fantasize about something hot, read a book (please, not if you're driving), listen to stimulating or silly podcasts, plan your ideal home, whatever. And on the way home be sure to include self-congratulatory thoughts about how well you did on your first day.

- Please, please, please **step away from your desk to eat lunch**. You've surely read the statistics about more bacteria on a typical desk than a public toilet. Unless you requested not to, your team has surely organized a welcome lunch.

- **Back at home** eat dinner at a leisurely pace and ask your partner to listen – without interrupting – to the story of your day. Ditch any chores not done by 8 p.m., have a couple of hours down-time, then get to bed.

Childcare

- **Your child is comfortable with his routine**, having been doing it for a few weeks, and is possibly looking forward to nursery/nanny/childminder so don't be clingy. If you have a nanny you probably don't need to do anything before leaving the house.

- If your child is cared for outside your home, **have your partner get her ready** this morning and tomorrow if possible. The next few days especially are about you and your transition, hence you should rally practical and emotional support to allow you to focus on meeting your needs. Ultimately the whole family wins when you settle back into work smoothly.

- **Talk about your day with enthusiasm** and ask about his day. Depending on your child's age he might not talk back but at least you're being bright, bubbly and giving the impression Mummy going out to work is good.

Exercise ✒
Advanced Planning

Buy yourself a week-to-view diary and use it to store to-do lists for a given week. Using the suggested schedule in this chapter as a starting point, write your task list for the weeks running up to your return, now. Remember, proper planning produces performance and things written down eases memory strain.

Make Your First Weekend a Mars Bar Weekend

I can't guarantee you won't need an energy boost at the end of your first week but I'm not about to advocate stuffing yourself with chocolate. In fact many working mums say they feel invigorated by being back amongst adults and doing something different with their noggins. The Mars Bar Weekend idea is about having time to 'work, rest and play' – the original Mars slogan. Mother-of-two Mathilde went with her children and husband to stay at the in-laws to get a good dose of rest and play:

It was a rest once we got there (having done the shopping and laundry before we went) and neither my husband nor I had to think about cooking, tidying up or anything routine. It was pure relaxed time together, which was a really good way to round off what was a great but tiring first week.

In the next chapter you'll find more on how to have restful, playful family weekends and still get the domestic must-dos done.

TRANSITIONING INTO WORKING MOTHERHOOD

I work with a lot of women who are on the brink of making significant changes in their lives. Transitioning from being primarily a carer for your child to being a parent with additional responsibilities outside the home is what psychologists deem a 'significant life event'. From the women I've worked with I've seen that those who keep other aspects of their lives as steady as possible – that is, who don't heap other changes on themselves at the same time – tend to fare best of all. You may well still be adjusting to becoming a mother, which is even more reason to go easy on yourself.

All this said, life can be like buses and sometimes we just have to get on with managing a newborn, a house-move and a partner's redundancy all at the same time.

Psychologists such as William Bridges (author of *Transitions: Making Sense of Life's Changes*, which I recommend if you're keen to know more about the psychology of change) have identified typical emotions and thought patterns associated with positive and negative life events. I won't go into depth about these here, but suffice to say the range of things you feel when adapting to a change is usually entirely normal. Even positive life events like getting married, being promoted and having a baby are associated with feelings of anxiety, questioning about whether we've done the right thing and whether life wasn't better before.

> 'In hindsight I wouldn't have accepted additional tasks so readily from my manager. He didn't really appreciate the extra hours required to do this nor the extra time I was having to spend working that detracted from my home life.'

Women I have coached say it's important to give yourself time to adapt to being a working mother, especially if things don't go quite the way you thought they would. Things may be easier or trickier than you imagined and, by building up slowly, reviewing how things are going and making any necessary adjustments at work and home, you are more likely to have a smooth transition. It's OK to feel what you're feeling, and you won't be the first to feel it.

In terms of work, having a performance plan or list of objectives for your first month will help you gauge how you're doing. If you feel in practice that what you thought looked all right on paper is placing an excessive burden on you, say so. By speaking up about how things are shaping up you appear confident and in control. The worst thing you can do is be silent, hope that problems will resolve themselves or try and carry on as though nothing is wrong.

Have that meeting with your boss to discuss how things are going and talk about any adjustments you think you need to make. Be as proactive as possible by suggesting where you go from here in terms of workload, projects and any new ideas you have. You are a fresh pair of eyes on the organization so what you have to say is even more valuable than it was before you left. At least that's the way enlightened people think about their women returners.

Here's some final food for thought from other mums:

- 'I have returned to work three times and each time it was hard initially but after only a few months I am settled and I'm sure it was the right decision for us. No harm in trying it, you can always do something else if it doesn't work out.'

- 'Hang in there for at least three months – it takes time to get used to being back at work and your new routine.'

- 'Accept it will be hard at first, as you have been with them 24/7 but you will get into a new routine where everyone is happy.'

- 'I found the first few weeks a real struggle, getting used to being back at work after a long break and getting used to being away from my children, even though it was only two days a week. It took a bit of time to adjust and I came close to resigning. After a few weeks, however, I got used to it all and I appreciate it more now.'

- 'If there have been any hiccups during the first month address the problem as soon as you can. Include your partner/parents/childminder/au pair in the discussion as you won't always have all the answers yourself.'

- 'Being a working mum is a "work in progress". It is not a destination but a journey that meanders through life with different pressures and pleasures as our children get older.'

KEY IDEAS & ACTION POINTS

The mum's mantra for this chapter is 'Prepare for a smooth return.'

- **Prepare for your return across four key areas of your life:** professional, personal, childcare and domestic duties.

- **Schedule what needs to be done** using a week-to-view diary as a place to write to-do lists rather than relying on your memory.

- **Go easy on yourself**, remembering you are adapting to a significant change in your life.

MUM'S MANTRA

8

Do What It Takes to Thrive

From surviving to thriving – how to become a flourishing family

Be kind to yourself. Don't waste what little time there is left over feeling bad – enjoy your children and be proud of yourself for all that you do.

HAYLEY, A WORKING MUM

A s a coach it's no wonder I like travel analogies, so let me repeat the wise words of the mum at the end of the last chapter: working motherhood is a journey, not a destination. It's important we working mums recognize this so we can garner the ongoing support and put systems in place to help our families flourish. The fact is, getting back to work and coping with the first week or month is just the beginning of things. To move from hanging-on-in-there-with-gritted-teeth to thriving needs a little more than we've talked about so far.

> *'It's quite hard to spot when you are "surviving" rather than living. Tell-tale signs are zero me time and less socializing with adults.'*

The mantra, then, for this final chapter is *Do what it takes to thrive*.

'Thriving' might seem like an impossibly big aspiration, but not if you keep your inner perfectionist locked up. The secret is not to expect every day to feel like a 'thriving' sort of a day. 'Survival' days are all part of life's rich tapestry, and so long as you're having more on-top than on-the-floor kinds of days, then you're doing it.

Along with uncovering the secrets to getting more me time and sleep time, in this final chapter you'll discover how to keep your family together, the relationship with your partner going strong and your work life satisfying.

THE PSYCHOLOGY OF CHANGE

Before we delve into the tested tips and tricks of the working mums who've gone before you, I'd like to say a bit more about the working motherhood journey.

In the previous chapter I said that with every major life transition people usually experience a similar sequence of thoughts and emotions. Psychologists studying how people cope with change find that even if we bring the change on ourselves and feel positive about it, we are likely to experience a feeling of complete regret and a sense of crisis at some point within three to nine months of returning to work. If this sounds depressing, don't worry! The 'crisis' may just be a moment or a day of feeling this way before you employ your coping strategies: giving yourself a good talking to, letting off steam with friends, and making time for something other than work and children are three of the most valued techniques used by women I coach.

> *'Working and using my brain gives me energy, makes me enjoy being me. Being a mother is great, but being only a mother would do my head in.'*

The point is, any life change – whether we view it as positive or negative – is a time of loss and upheaval as well as a time of excitement. We are letting go of one way of doing things and embracing something new. We need to give ourselves time to adjust, and knowing that we may feel down, confused or upset even several months on from going back to work can be helpful. That's why I think it's worth repeating this nugget of wisdom from a working mum: 'Hang on in there for at least three months because things take time to settle down. There will be bumps along the way, guaranteed, even if you got off to a good start.'

WHAT SUCCESSFUL FAMILIES DO

In 2001, US researchers led by Shelley Haddock studied the lives of nearly 50 middle-class dual-earner couples who were successfully managing work and children. They discovered that these successful couples structure their lives around 10 major strategies:

1. valuing family

2. striving for partnership

3. deriving meaning from work

4. maintaining work boundaries

5. focusing and producing at work

6. taking pride in dual earning

7. prioritizing family fun

8. living simply

9. making decisions proactively

10. valuing time.

Of course, like much excellent research this confirms what we probably knew already. Knowing is one thing, remembering to live it is another. I stick lists like this up in my kitchen as a daily reminder. I've also added an eleventh strategy which I was staggered not to see already: 'Me time'. How on earth can we thrive without that?

THRIVE WITH A HOBBY AND TIME TO YOURSELF

I believe that a happy mother makes a happy home; we cannot take care of others without taking care of ourselves first. For this reason I'm happy to go so far as to say it's selfish *not* to have me time. Is this radical? Not if we're all being honest.

What does 'me time' mean to you? And how are you going to get it? Take a minute to think about how you can carve out pockets of time to do three things for yourself each day. They may only be small things but they contribute to your well-being.

On top of this, think about how you can create room to pursue an interest beyond work and family once a week. From singing with Rock Choir and scrapbooking to college courses, 'Pop Dance' and meditation, the working mums who've been where you are now say having a hobby is part of thriving. It might be easier to make time for a defined activity than a soak in the bath as this mum says:

When my daughter was about 18 months old I did some evening classes. Everyone knew it was my college night so if my husband wasn't home then one of my parents would make sure they were here to babysit. If I had just said to my husband I would like two hours every Thursday evening to myself with no responsibility for the children it would not always have happened. But college nights were definitely mine – clever, eh?!

REFRAME YOUR PERCEPTIONS OF ME TIME

I asked 50 working mums for their opinions on what it takes to thrive. I asked how much 'me time' they have each week, what they do with it and why. What was really interesting was the interpretation of 'me time', since some mums quoted up to 24 hours a week whilst others could only muster 60 minutes every seven days ('I have approximately one hour a week and I lie in the bath with a glass of wine and shave my legs at the same time.'). I'm hoping the mother who wrote 'What???' did in fact have some down-time every day but didn't interpret it as 'me time'. I'm afraid slumping in front of the telly because you feel too knackered to do anything else (as many mothers confess) definitely *is* me time. And that's official: the grandfather of time-use research in the US, Professor John Robinson, has done the research. According to Robinson's analysis of 427 dual-earner families' time diaries, mothers had 33.8 hours' free time a week and fathers 35.8.

> *'I used to regard "me time" as a luxury but – nearly 11 years (how did that happen?!) into parenthood and three children – I know it's a NECESSITY. It's a sanity-saver and makes me feel like ME again. It doesn't take much – I think being a mum you're easily pleased, but it's amazing how even a quick coffee by yourself or a long soak in the bath with a glass of wine can revive your spirits.'*

If you're about to screech with incredulity that the man is a fool, you've got to cut Robinson some slack when you read that he doesn't class many of the things most of us find pleasurable (like baking kids' birthday cakes, getting our hair cut, playing with our children and doing the ironing whilst enjoying the radio) as leisure activities. Neither does he count reading your book whilst commuting as leisure time but, as this mum explains, she does:

Once the children have gone to bed and I've finished supper, tidying, online grocery shopping, etc., I've got about 30 minutes to myself before I need to go to bed.

I like to just zone out with a book or a TV show. I have started to count my train journey to work as 'me time' to try to psychologically redress the balance. I use my half-hour journey to listen to an audio book, which is pure escapism.

> 'As a couple we are good at looking ahead to where the pressure points are going to be and helping each other out. When my non-school days are filled with freelance work, we share things much more. The other important factor is to give each other time for themselves. This might just be going for a run, meeting friends or a night or two away with a friend or family. Everyone in the family unit benefits from this time.'

If you feel you don't have as much me time as you want/need/feel you deserve, there are two things you can do. One is to deliberately cut down on things you don't want to do so you can take time back for yourself. The other, possibly easier option, is to recognize the pleasure you get from the things you already do and reframe it as me time. *The Times* newspaper columnist Caitlin Moran once quipped that as a parent she's subjugated her desires for so long it feels like she's treating herself when she folds up and puts away towels. I know that feeling of despair, but on the other hand, because I love to cook I see making the family dinner as leisure time – so long as I'm left alone to do it.

A final thought on me time is that it's not the hours you get that count but your perception that you're getting sufficient time to yourself. The need for me time ebbs and flows according to what's going on in our lives, and so long as we can make arrangements to get it when we need it, we're winning. If you're living the working mum's Mantra #3, See Your Family as a Team, it shouldn't be too hard to get the time you need for an hour's peace and quiet, a soak in the tub, a gym class or whatever makes you feel rested and relaxed.

'Don't try to do everything. It really doesn't matter if you're late for work every now and again, or you miss your train, or you forget that it's dress-up day at nursery. The key is to prioritize. Don't get too caught up in the minutiae of your schedule. Things will change and you must be flexible. If you tie yourself to a strict schedule, and miss something, you'll create unnecessary stress on yourself and your family. RELAX!'

THRIVE BY REFINING YOUR JUGGLING ACT

There's a well-pedalled life-balance analogy that likens our family, friends, health and career to balls we juggle every day. The first three are made of glass and our career is made of rubber. Drop the glass and it's changed forever, drop the rubber and it will bounce back. It's a nice idea, but I don't agree that our friends, family and health can't bounce back if we take our eye off them, or that our career necessarily will if we do. However, the sentiment is a nice reminder to get some perspective if we feel overwhelmed or stressed by work. The anecdote is attributed to the then-CEO of Coca-Cola, Brian Dyson. The speech he gave in 1996 signalled his belief in numbers 1, 4, 5 and 10 of the list of things thriving families do which I mentioned at the beginning of this chapter. Can you imagine how much easier working motherhood would be with someone like that for a boss? There's more on thriving at work later in the chapter.

'My partner and I are doing our best to make sure we have more time together, so have decided to go out together at least once a month. Whatever rows or upsets we've had through the day, we

all kiss and hug each other to say goodnight. And, if we've had a particularly fraught day, our family mantra is: "Tomorrow is another day."'

PRIORITIZE YOUR CLOSEST RELATIONSHIP

Bosses aside, we all need someone beyond work to support us emotionally. The obvious place to turn is to your partner. As this dad, Sam, says:

Sometimes my wife feels the pressure at work and we have a good chat about it. I sometimes have to put things into perspective for her and remind her that other people have far worse problems i.e. like not having a roof over your head and major debt.

'Another golden rule I'd like to reinstal (not been able to this year with a new baby) is to have about three days' holiday/a long weekend without the children every year.'

As two people choosing to be partners in life, you should be each other's biggest champions and primary sources of strength. You are what makes life wonderful for the other and together you are the foundation of your family. Because of this you owe it to your children to get a babysitter once a week and go out to dinner. And to have the occasional weekend away, if not *frequent* weekends away. It would be selfish not to. Think about your mummy network and whom you can reciprocate with if you haven't got family or the means to pay someone to babysit.

As well as sumptuous dinners and delicious weekends, there's an excellent, easy, free thing you can do every day to keep your relationship thriving: positive talk. Sex works as well, for sure, but feeling a daily obligation is definitely a passion killer. Heaven help any woman who ever puts love-making on her to-do list.

Marital stability expert and psychologist Dr John Gottman has analysed the behaviour of thousands of couples (gay and straight) and found it's possible to predict with a high degree of accuracy the relationships that will survive and those that will end, by the ratio of positive to negative comments that pass between them. The magic formula is 5:1 in relationships that last. What's also telling is the way a couple argues and resolves conflict. Having kids can put pressure on a relationship like you've never experienced before, so it's worth choosing your battles, using humour and trying to see your partner's perspective to cool things down. A bit like the parenting books suggest we do with our kids.

THRIVING FAMILY HABITS

Keen to get a sense of what working parents think helps their family stay happy and healthy, I asked 50 mothers about any golden rules they have at home.

Mealtimes Matter

Around half of the mums mentioned the importance of family mealtimes, saying the ideal is to eat at least one meal together at a table every day. Apart from mealtimes being an opportunity to talk (or babble), eating together also helps our children learn good food habits. But is it always easy to eat together every day? Probably not, given the fact one parent often leaves early to be back in time for end of day pick-ups and the other goes late so they can do the morning drop-off. 'Ships passing in the night' or 'tag-team' is the way some parents describe the early years. Despite this, many families do manage to have an early breakfast or late dinner together most days. Weekends are the perfect time to bond over food, as Maggie says:

Sunday is family day, and very social. After we sit down to eat, we discuss the following week, so that we all know who is doing what and when. My older children often help with cooking, and we all plan meals for the week. We have one child who is very much a carnivore, and another who is almost veggie, so we try to keep everybody happy! We can plan for any extra dinner guests, too - evening mealtimes are the only time we are all together, so it's really important to us.

'We try to have at least one day every weekend that it's just us – no other family or friends around. Obviously, if people are coming to visit for the weekend, or if we have to travel to see the rest of the family, this doesn't apply (one of the many disadvantages of not having family living nearby); but otherwise, we try and have this "family day" to do things just by ourselves. We keep it fairly spontaneous, as we might change plans according to the weather or how we are feeling.'

Weekend Double Act

When our son was coming up to two-and-a-half and our daughter nearly six months old, I was desperate for more time to myself. Fed up with the constraints of breastfeeding and ground down by sleepless winter nights, there were moments when I was ready to shell out my life savings on a live-in nanny or else flog both children on eBay to finance my running away. Luckily it didn't come to that, as my husband suggested I have a Saturday off every fortnight.

According to the 'Fathers, Family and Work' report from the UK Equality and Human Rights Commission, 62 per cent of fathers think that dads should spend more time caring for their children. My husband is in the other 38 per cent, but it didn't stop him from seeing my plight and stepping in. I was so buoyed by having six hours as a free agent I suggested we take this day off in turns.

When I shared what I thought was a stroke of genius with mums around me, the reaction was less positive than I expected. 'But that's a whole day out of family time' they were saying – so here's the moral of the story: every family needs to do different things to thrive, so be careful with your comparisons. The mums who balked at us having alternate Saturdays off typically had husbands who didn't see much of them or their kids during the week. In contrast, both Nick and I are generally in to eat with our children and do bathtime together three out of five weekday nights plus weekends. When you add up this regular and frequent family time, we didn't feel under as much pressure as some families to milk every moment of the weekend.

As it turned out, the alternate Saturdays 'off' only lasted a couple of months because breastfeeding ended, sleep returned and winter turned to spring. In short, we weren't the desperate people we *had* been, so things could change again. That's another valuable lesson: thriving is as much about testing and tweaking family rules as it is about having them in the first place.

> *My husband and I also take turns to have a lie-in on the weekend. I generally get up on Saturday morning and then have a lie-in on Sundays. No matter how many chores there are, we always have a family trip out at some point on the weekend.*

American researchers (Milkie *et al.*, 2004), studying the feelings of parents about time spent with their children, found that nearly half of the parents residing with their children feel they spend too little time with them. Unsurprisingly, the more hours worked, the greater this feeling. However, as other academics studying maternal guilt report (for example Bianchi, 2000), parents today spend the same amount of time or more with the children than in the past. In short, you're normal to feel time-strain, but your littlies are not hard done by – so let go of the guilt!

To make the most of family time, many of the mums who shared their golden rules talked about 'ring-fencing' a Saturday or Sunday to have fun as a family without outsiders. Others said it helps them to split the weekend into a day for getting the jobs done and a day to get out together, as Samantha says:

> weekend time is family time and we do stuff together and avoid going to the supermarket if at all possible. We try to preserve Sundays as family day and usually go on a big walk for fresh air, exercise and a chance to talk.

Get Enough Sleep

I don't know about you, but I rarely get to wake up when I'm ready these days. Early nights happen often but still my body craves an extra few minutes in the morning and the chance to come round properly before the demands for banana, drinks and Lego-building come at me. Cue weekend lie-in swapsies:

> Usually my husband has Saturday morning with my son so I get a lie-in to catch up and some time to organize myself. We do not have any rules though, although we never make plans at the weekend without consulting each other.

My husband and I take it in turns to have a lie-in Saturday/Sunday, for survival really due to lack of sleep. It means we never eat breakfast as a family, though, but sleep is more important at the moment.

While a weekend lie-in may be a nice-to-have for some, it can be essential to mothers and fathers of very young children or those with children who have problematic sleeping habits. Postnatal maternal mood disorder and problems with children's sleep behaviour are common in the first year, and researchers say there is a clear association between the two. Prior to 1998, when a group of Australian doctors published results of their childhood sleep-modification programme, it was believed that postnatal depression could be the cause of an infant's sleep problems and not the other way around. Their research turned this on its head, showing that with improvements in a child's sleep can come an improvement in the mother. As they caution in their research paper published in *The Journal of Paediatric Child Health*, there is the possibility that mothers have been receiving ineffective or even harmful treatment for postnatal depression when in fact the remedy for their depressed mood is simply more sleep.

While this book is not intended as a guide to raising kids, I can say from personal experience and talking to many other parents that it really does pay to kick unwanted sleep habits into touch as soon as you can – be those your own bad habits (watching TV in bed, too much alcohol or caffeine before sleep, not getting to bed early enough to name just three) or your child's. I can recall the difference in myself on days when I'd had good kip and the days following a couple of bad nights. Sleep deprivation could make me tearful, anxious, on edge and without my usual confidence. This is clearly not a good state to be in at work or at home. We've never had our children in bed with us in the night and we've been through

difficult periods when we've used controlled crying techniques to get them to stay in bed and sleep. It worked for us.

A good indicator that you're getting enough sleep is
waking up naturally. On the days when you've had enough
sleep, can you recall how you achieved it? If sleep is an issue
for you it's worth keeping a sleep diary and experimenting
with sleeping arrangements and routines to get a good
night's kip more of the time. If lack of sleep is due to a baby
or problem sleeper, focus your sleep diary and experimenting on them. A Lumie alarm clock for a gentle waking is a
nice touch, too, especially in the winter.

Enjoy Simple Pleasures with Children

One of the things I still marvel at – in addition to the amazing effects of a good night's sleep – is how much pleasure
children get from simple things. Take the cardboard box at
Christmas by way of an example. This facet of our children
is a huge boon but, sadly, not enough of us capitalize on it.
Given that simple living and valuing family time are two of
the 10 strategies thriving working families employ, simple
fun sounds like the answer at weekends. Instead many of us
try and do too much on non-work days, probably to assuage
the feelings of guilt around not spending every waking hour
with our little ones. But there's no need, because the thing
our children want most in the world is our attention and
involvement in what they're doing. It's not by chance that
one of our youngest child's first sentences was 'Mummy
sit down.' Put simply, 'quality time' can happen anywhere,
anytime, so long as we're in the mood for it.

Don't 'Permatain' Your Children

Author of the hilarious parenting book *The Idle Parent*, Tom
Hodgkinson declares that our kids are better off when we

'don't waste money on family days out and holidays ... we play in the fields and forests ... we fill the house with music and merriment ... we read them poetry and fantastic stories.' These ideas all embrace the idea that simplicity is good. If you've read any of Hodgkinson's work you'll know he's the antithesis of the 'helicopter parent' – a fan of the hands-off-and-leave-them-alone school of parenting.

> *'I did what worked for my family. In hindsight I should have put my own needs first much sooner.'*
> **WINIFRED ROBINSON, BBC** PRESENTER

In a similar vein, I think a lot of working parents, driven by guilt and perceived societal values, fall into the trap of what I call 'permataining' their children. That's short for *permanently entertaining*. Taking an interest and joining in with what our children are doing is one thing, but being ever present and directive reduces their capacity for resourcefulness. And whilst you're busy permataining you can't be doing the other things that help you and your family to thrive. Play is just one part of a happy family and 'little and often' is a good mantra.

The majority of parents I've ever spoken to do not derive as much pleasure from building spaceships, pretending to be farmyard animals or role-playing with plastic dolls and fuzzy bears as they would have onlookers believe. It takes a confident parent to admit this publicly, but that's not necessary: private recognition of what you do and don't enjoy about being a parent makes it easier to have good times, more of the time.

Play to Your Strengths

Life feels better when we play to our strengths rather than focusing on correcting perceived weaknesses. Transferring this idea to parenting, what kind of play comes easily to you? What do you enjoy doing with your baby and older children? Baking buns, chasing them with the Dyson, digging for worms, pulling weeds and running races are all on my play list. Ask me to do imaginary play and I last five minutes.

Given that children have a huge repertoire of things they enjoy, it makes sense to encourage them towards the things we can derive pleasure from, too. Then we all have a good time. For sure as children grow we want them to develop their own tastes and preferences, but where's the rule that says these things can't be what we like, too? It feels good to share an interest and, as the saying goes, those that play together, stay together. This is a great sentiment for family life.

Play Together

Depending on the age of your children you might like to organize weekend plans together. Since our son was about three I've made a point of asking him what he'd like to do this coming weekend – and at the same time tell him what Mummy and Daddy would like to do. When everyone gets a say it keeps us all happy. The other bonus is that our son usually comes out with something simple and, because it's what the boy's asked for, I don't need to feel guilty about not doing something totally whizz-bang like the seaside or the zoo.

Exercise ✐
Your Thrive Audit

If you want to thrive you need to know where you're doing well already and where to focus extra attention. This Thrive Audit will help you do this. If you use it before or in the first few weeks of returning to work, you should then also complete it again after a couple of months when being a working mum is business as usual.

Below is a series of statements that relate to different areas of your life. Read each one and respond by putting a number against each as follows:

1 = strongly disagree, **2** = disagree, **3** = neutral, **4** = agree, **5** = strongly agree

No one else needs to see this, so do yourself and your family a favour by going with your gut feel – it's usually right.

Self	Your Rating
Most days I spend some time doing what I want to do.	
I have a hobby or interest I regularly do.	
I wake refreshed most days.	
Most days I get some exercise.	
I regularly spend time with some of my closest friends .	
I feel positive at the moment and optimistic about the future.	
	TOTAL
Partner	
We regularly talk to one another about things that interest us.	
The last time we went out just the two of us was less than a month ago.	
We have sex and intimate moments about as much as we'd both like.	
We often say kind and supportive things to each other.	
We regularly make each other laugh and smile.	
We have a shared outlook on parenting and family life.	
	TOTAL
Family	
We eat together at least once a day.	
I do something playful with my child(ren) every day.	
We have special time all together at least once a week.	
I play to my strengths when I play with my child(ren).	
We strike a good balance between time on chores and time for play.	

My child seems to enjoy the daycare arrangements I've made.	
	TOTAL
Work	
I take pride and feel there is purpose in my work.	
I work in a supportive environment.	
I have a mentor and/or do things to develop myself at work.	
On balance my work hours and commute do not have an adverse affect.	
I stick to boundaries I put in place at work.	
On the whole I play to my strengths at work.	
	TOTAL

If you scored 30 in each box, congratulations, you are officially amazing! If you scored 25–29 in a particular section you are probably thriving in this area of your life. If you scored less than 24 in any area, look at the individual items you scored three or less for. These are areas to focus on.

If you're really keen to set yourself and your family up to thrive, take a look at each item you scored three or less for and answer these questions:

1. **What is the nub of this issue?**

2. **What positive steps have you taken in the past that could give you a higher score here and now?**

3. **What *could* you do to get a higher score?**

4. **What *will* you do to get a higher score?**

THRIVE AT WORK

From play at home to fun at work: many of the mums I've talked to say that, unless you absolutely have to work to pay your basic bills it's really not worth returning unless you enjoy it and it makes financial sense. Given that there's usually a cost to working (a friend recently had to quit a job she enjoyed on having her second child because it was going to cost £150/day in travel and childcare) it's really important the numbers add up. Thriving at work clearly involves earning a fair wage for what you do. Are you earning what you are worth? What the market says is the going rate? If salary negotiations are on your mind you might want to reread the section in the Mantra #2 chapter on asking for what you want.

> *'I miss my little girl all the time but I know it was the right decision for us. I think it's really important to enjoy what you do so that it feels like it makes sense.'*

I believe thriving at work also entails these items from the 'what successful families do' list I mentioned at the beginning of this chapter:

- deriving meaning from work

- maintaining work boundaries

- focusing and producing at work.

DERIVING MEANING FROM WORK

What do you get from the work you do? What boxes does going to work tick? When you've settled back into your role, these things may start to change. You might want something more or something different to what motivated you before. As a working mum there'll always be a pull between work and home life, and whilst many mums report wanting to stretch and develop themselves at work, they worry about the price they'll pay at home. As Lisa says:

Keep your eye on the old work/life balance. It's very easy to be seduced by work. You're back to your old self, in control, receiving praise and recognition ... It's very easy to turn a blind eye to your home becoming a pig-sty, your children becoming feral and your relationship being reduced to grunts and nods.

> *'When you develop yourself, you develop your family.'*

If you enjoy your work for 70–80 per cent of the time or would give yourself 7/8 out of 10 overall for work satisfaction, you're doing well. Any more and you really are in an enviable position. Any less and it's probably time to consider moving to new challenges or tweaking your existing role to play to more of your strengths more often. When people call me and say they're fed up with work they've previously been happy with, I ask them to think about what they would need to do to make it good again. It's surprising how simple it can be to turn a jaded work experience around.

Get a Mentor

Of the 150 women I surveyed on reasons for returning to work, 79 per cent said they were looking forward to the opportunities for personal growth, and 91 per cent to using their skills again. If I could give you only one piece of advice about thriving at work it would be to get a mentor who understands your current priorities and whom you view as a role model. A mentor is someone whose experiences you can benefit from to develop yourself. They may be internal or external, male or female; the important thing is that they inspire you and are keen to support you. It's up to you to seek out that person and share what it is you hope you can learn from them. In my experience, most people are incredibly flattered to be asked and *will* say yes. Incidentally, in their book *Coaching Women to Lead*, Averil Leimon and her co-authors cite 'networking' and 'role models' as two of the most important strategies for women getting on at work.

Get a Coach

Like a mentor, a coach can be a source of inspiration and support during periods of change, and can help you find solutions to specific problems. Whilst a mentor is usually focused on professional development, a coach can help you more widely with transition into motherhood and working parenthood. Switched-on organizations get people like me and my team in to deliver 'women returner' programmes which include one-to-one coaching, workshops and 'Keep In Touch' networking events for women on maternity leave and recent returners. As a study published in the *International Journal of Evidence Based Coaching and Mentoring* concludes:

> If employers are to support women through the shifting phases of this transition, they need to put in place measures that can support them. Coaching offers an appropriate and objective framework for women returning to meet the challenge of realigning work expectations and priorities.

Working-mums-to-be also call me directly before they go back to work; typical reasons include: confidence being at a low ebb (so we work on ways to boost it); being uncertain about whether to go back and, if so, to what kind of work (so we lay out the options and mull them over until she finds clarity); feeling unsure about job applications and interviews (so we polish and practise together); knowing she wants to work for herself but not knowing at what or how (so we look at her talents, let our imaginations run wild, weigh up the options and create a plan of action) and so on. Similarly, mums who are back at work call me and say things like, 'Help, I feel like I'm drowning,' 'I'm knackered and can't go on like this,' 'I want to move jobs but I'm scared I won't find part-time work,' 'I'm bored' and 'I feel so guilty.' Together we work it out.

MAINTAINING WORK BOUNDARIES

In the second chapter I talked about maintaining work boundaries. Did you do the 'Your Work–Home Boundaries' exercise (see page 87)? I think it's worth recapping that, while boundaries are good for us, it's normal to get frustrated by the limits they impose on us, for example the feeling that we're never able to give as much to anything as we'd like. Even with determined boundary-setting work sometimes creeps into home, home impacts on work (23 per cent of the mums I surveyed said they spend 50 per cent or more of their day thinking about their kids) and sometimes we rant that we're fed up of being jack of all trades and master of none. But without boundaries we'd be even more stressed, I'm sure.

I was running a workshop at BT and a manager shared the story of a technically brilliant woman who works for him. He said she takes on too much and tries to do everything to a higher standard than is really needed. He was concerned that this meant she wasn't going to hit the team's targets, but more than this he was bothered for her health and family's sake. He told me she's got to be comfortable about drawing boundaries and reflected that maybe he needed to alter the balance of praise he gives for 'perfect work' versus sticking to boundaries in order to bring about a change in her. A true and thoughtful reflection. If you didn't do the exercise in chapter two about boundaries, why not pop back and get really confident on how to manage the balance between work and home, now?

FOCUSING AND PRODUCING AT WORK

Shelly Haddock and co-researchers at Colorado University interviewed 50 dual-earning couples and found that focusing and being productive at work are crucial to successful family life. It also makes leaving the office without a backward glance much easier to do. These comments from mothers and fathers sum up why and how they do it:

M: 'We're both pulling our weight at our jobs. No one has ever felt that we're slacking off or we're getting off easy because we've got kids. We're in there and doing more than what they've asked us to do. That's how we keep options open.'

F: 'I think that if you're good at what you do, they will accept those boundaries. They won't question you because the quality of your work is good. I see them questioning other people but I believe that's because they're questioning the quality of their work. They get a lot of work out of me.'

M: 'We both like our jobs, but, when it's quitting time, we're out of there. I mean with both our jobs you could work 24 hours a day; it's a neverending workload.'

F: 'I don't mess around. When I'm there, I'm working. I'm not chatting: I'm working. And I think that's key. You just try to be really efficient and be on form when you're there.'

M: 'With the person I'm working for now when she says "Oh, here's a project, I'd like you to do it," instead of saying "Yeah I'll just do it," I say "OK, I can do that but I need four weeks." Because I know I'm not going to work on Saturdays or after 5 p.m.'

How can you be more focused and productive at work? I'm sure you've got some good strategies already – here are three more:

1. The night before the first day of your working week, write a list of priorities for the week ahead and draw a line under it. If other things crop up during the week write them below the line and make a conscious choice as to whether they should take precedence over the things you considered the most important at the start of the week.

2. Choose three main priorities each day, write them on a post-it note and stick it somewhere prominent. Completing those gives you license to feel good and guilt-free about leaving for the day.

3. Keep a list of short, simple tasks (what I call 'five-minute fillers') alongside your weekly priority list and do these when your energy is waning. Five-minute fillers are good things to do between your concentration-intensive tasks but never at the start of the day when you're fresh.

Manage Your Energy

To be focused and productive you need to take breaks and have lunch. Chocolate biscuits are optional, fresh air is not.

When on maternity leave, how often have you hoped to eat your lunch in peace instead of being pestered, interrupted or whined at? (I'm thinking about your children rather than your colleagues here.) Going back to work is the perfect opportunity to bring this small indulgence to life, and dozens of mothers tell me this is one of their work-day highlights. In your first fortnight you might begin with good intentions and make time for the staff canteen, a team lunch, a stroll round the block or the shops or maybe a quick gym sesh. Given how good it feels to take a break and relish eating in peace, how will you keep it up and steer clear of the must-keep-going-got-loads-to-do-before-nursery-pick-up mentality? Think about it now and you're more likely to stick to it.

> 'Being French, meals have always been important. Logically I should really enjoy the days I am at work and can have a lunch and do whatever I want but what happens is I get so into my work that I actually hardly ever go out to eat something and enjoy myself. Now, don't get me wrong, I will always get something to eat and have a break, but it's at my desk most of the time. Do I feel annoyed with myself? Yes. Because then I think, I wish I had gone out and had 'paused' for a while, for a little time of self-reflection, rather than sitting at my desk and risk being disturbed or interrupted by colleagues.'

There's a heck of a lot of extra time being put in by the whole UK workforce, not just mothers, as a result of not taking lunch. According to consumer research by SPAR in 2009, around seven million workers skip their lunch break, and more than 70 per cent of the UK workforce do not leave their desk to eat. It can be tempting to forgo your lunch break and carry on through your to-do list for the sense of satisfaction you have at the end of it, but consider these five compelling reasons to take a break, from nutritional therapist, Kim Crundall:

1. If you always eat lunch your blood sugar levels will remain more constant throughout the afternoon, particularly if you always eat a protein food source with some carbohydrate. This means your energy levels are higher and your concentration is better – therefore you're likely to achieve more.

2. Low blood-sugar levels don't just affect your concentration, they affect your mood, too, often leaving people snappy and irritable. Having time out for lunch will actually make you feel more able to cope with unexpected demands, and your colleagues will appreciate your better mood.

3. Eating at your desk leaves you focused on other tasks; to your body, doing your own personal emails or phone calls is no different from work emails or phone calls. It locks you into the 'fight or flight' response so your body can't switch off.

4. Taking a break, even for 15–20 minutes, de-stresses your body, switching off your 'fight or flight' response. You then digest your food better and feel more energized going back to work.

5. Look at having a lunch break as an investment; the time out pays you back in terms of energy levels and productivity. And the big bonus is that you'll leave work having some surplus energy to invest in your family.

Go into Neutral on the Way Home

Anja says she finds the hardest part of being a working mum is having no time between work and home. 'The second I get home I'm Mummy again. I'd love a bit of down-time first, which their dad gets as I'm home first.'

> *'Plan your day so it gives you "me" time – even if it's just 30 minutes a day. Take a quick power nap in your car if you can.'*

This is where public transport and/or extendable childcare come into their own. If you let the bus, tram or train take the strain you can zone out to music, disengage with a podcast or get lost in a book. As with driving, going into neutral before changing from work gear to home gear helps everything happen much more smoothly.

Julie has a nanny who stays an hour later than usual one night a week so she can go for a swim on her way home: 'I feel better knowing at least once a week I'm going to have a break after work and fit exercise in that I probably wouldn't if I came home first.'

Even just a couple of minutes with your eyes closed before you put your mummy hat on can be a refresher – or, as mum-of-school-age-children Maggie says:

If you've had a challenging day, it's OK to say to your children – 'I love you, but give me half an hour for a cuppa and then you can tell me all about your day.' It can be so difficult to switch from working woman to home mum in a few minutes – allow yourself time. By setting boundaries, and being honest, your children will learn a fantastic example.

Exercise ✒

Your Thrive Manifesto

If, like me, you're one of those people who always skips the exercises in books like this, please make an exception for this one. I promise it will be worth it.

- Grab a piece of paper and write the numbers 1–10 equally spaced out down one side.

- Pick out any of the tips and ideas in this chapter that you really like and write one per space.

- Now jot down any other golden rules you already live by or would like to live by.

- Hey, presto! You have your personal 'Thrive Manifesto' to stick on your fridge.

- Feel free to embellish with bottle tops, stickers, tissue paper and signatures to make it a whole family thing.

KEY IDEAS & ACTION POINTS

The working mum's mantra for this chapter is 'Do what it takes to thrive.'

- **Remember, 'me time' is a necessity, not a luxury**, so do something for yourself daily and create time for a hobby outside work and family.

- **Prioritize your partner** and live the magic ratio of 5:1 positive to negative comments for a thriving relationship.

- **Create some good family habits** and stick to them – mealtimes matter, as does simple family fun.

- **Be focused and productive at work** by prioritizing three things each day and sticking to your boundaries.

- **Get a coach and find a mentor** to help you through the transition into working motherhood and inspire your professional development.

- **Prepare your thrive manifesto** and keep it somewhere visible as a daily reminder of what it takes to be a thriving working family.

Afterword

As I said in my Introduction, I believe work and parenting can be combined in a satisfying and rewarding way. I hope you feel equipped and empowered to do this after reading my thoughts, the stories of other working parents and the sprinkling of psychology findings I included too.

One of the best research findings I ever read – because of its simplicity and common sense apart from anything else – is the psychological benefit of writing down three good things each day and why they happened.

As working mothers it can be easy to lose sight of how rich and wonderful our lives are with young children in them. My mother-in-law always tells me these days are gone in a flash, even if they can feel long and difficult at the time. If there's one last piece of advice I can share with you, it's to write those three good things down every day. The act of writing can turn a troubled day on its head, rereading them when you're feeling down can give you a boost and revisiting them when you're 94 will surely give you a lot of pleasure as you remember that these days were some of the best of your life.

Yours with love, confidence and optimism,

Jessica

P.S. Join the Mothers Work! Facebook page and sign up for my free monthly thoughts to help you flourish: www.jessicachivers.com

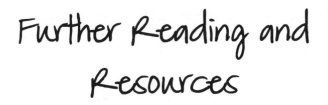

Further Reading and Resources

CHAPTER 1

R. C. Bartnett and C. Rivers, *She Works, He Works: How Two Income Families are Happier, Healthier and Better-off* (HarperCollins, 1996)

C. E. Bird and C.E. Ross, 'House workers and paid workers: qualities of the work and effects on personal control', *Journal of Marriage and the Family* 55 (1993): 913-25

S. Connolly and M. Gregory, 'The part-time pay penalty: earnings trajectories of British Women', *Oxford Economic Papers* 61 (2009): 176-97

Netmums Survey (2005) retrieved from: www.netmums.com/campaigns/The_Great_Work_Debate.341/

Christina Odone, *What Women Want* (Centre for Policy Studies, 2009)

C. E. Ross and J. Mirowsky, 'Does employment affect health?', *Journal of Health and Social Behavior* 36 (1995): 230-43

J. Schnittker, 'Working more and feeling better: women's health, employment and family life, 1974-2004', *American Sociological Review* 72 (2004): 221-38

The experiences of women returning to work after maternity leave in the UK: A summary of survey results produced by The NCT/Working Families. (Research led by Liz Morris, Aston Business School).

C. M. Thomas, 'Cost of depression among adults in England in 2000', *The British Journal of Psychiatry* 183 (2003): 514-19

US Department of Labor, 'Employment characteristics of families', press release April 20, 2004. Retrieved from stats.bls.gov/news.release/pdf/famee.pdf

CHAPTER 2

L. Babcock and S. Laschever, *Women Don't Ask: Negotiation and the Gender Divide* (Princeton University Press, 2003)

Changing Times from The TUC is a monthly online newsletter concerning work/life balance issues and legislation: www.tuc.org.uk/work_life

Department for Work and Pensions survey, 'Caring and Flexible Working': www.dwp.gov.uk/newsroom/press-releases/2009/july-2009/dwp027-09-310709.shtml

The experiences of women returning to work after maternity leave in the UK: A summary of survey results produced by The NCT/Working Families (research led by Liz Morris, Aston Business School)

M. Fine-Davis, J. Fagnani, D. Giovannini, L. Hojgaard and H. Clarke, 'Fathers and Mothers: Dilemmas of the Work-Life Balance', *Social Indicators Research Series*, 2004

E. J. Hill, A.J. Hawkins, M. Ferris and M. Weitzman, 'Finding an extra day a week: The positive influence of perceived job flexibility on work and family life balance', *Family Relations* 50 (2001): 49-58

NICE *Promoting mental well-being at work* guidelines available at guidance.nice.org.uk/PH22

CHAPTER 3

M. Fine-Davis, J. Fagnani, D. Giovannini, L. Hojgaard and H. Clarke, 'Fathers and Mothers: Dilemmas of the Work-Life Balance', *Social Indicators Research Series*, 2004

CHAPTER 4

www.babycentre.co.uk has a brilliant level of detail about the advantages and disadvantages of different forms of childcare

Children's Information Service information at www.child-carelink.gov.uk

Allison Lee, *The Parent's Guide to Choosing Childcare* (How to Books Ltd, 2008)

Nanny earnings information statistics retrieved June 30th 2010 from www.nannytax.co.uk/parents/employment-costs/the-nannytax-wages-survey/survey2009

National Childminding Association, www.ncma.org.uk, 0845 880 0044 – has a short film showcasing how childminders work and the benefits for families

Ofsted reports on nurseries, pre-schools, childminders and registered nannies at www.ofsted.gov.uk. Ofsted overall gradings provided by way of personal correspondence with the Ofsted Information Access Team, July 2010.

CHAPTER 5

Louann Brizendine, *The Female Brain* (Bantam, 2006)

Ylva Elvin-Nowak and Helene Thomsson, 'Motherhood as idea and practice: A discursive understanding of employed mothers in Sweden', *Gender and Society* 15 (2001): 407-28

Jackie Guendouzi, '''The Guilt Thing'': Balancing Domestic and Professional Roles', *Journal of Marriage and the Family* 68 (2006): 901-909

National Childbirth Trust information on combining breast-feeding and work retrieved from www.nct.org.uk/info-centre/how-do-i/view-79 on June 7th 2010

CHAPTER 6

C. Bird, 'Gender, Household Labor and Psychological Distress: The Impact of the Amount and Division of Housework', *Journal of Health and Social Behavior* 40 (1999): 32-45

Jamie Oliver, *Jamie's 30-Minute Meals* (Michael Joseph, 2010)

Karen Pine and Simonne Gnessen, *Sheconomics* (Headline, 2009)

CHAPTER 7

William Bridges, *Transitions: Making Sense of Life's Changes* (Da Capo, 2004)

Allison Mitchell, *Time Management for Manic Mums* (Hay House, 2006)

Richard Wiseman, *The Luck Factor* (Arrow Books, 2004)

CHAPTER 8

K. L. Armstrong, A. R. Van Haeringen, M.R. Dadds and R. Cash, 'Sleep deprivation or post-natal depression in later infancy: Separating the chicken from the egg', *Journal of Paediatric Child Health* 34 (1998): 260-62

S. M. Bianchi, 'Maternal employment and time with children: Dramatic change or surprising continuity?', *Demography* 37 (2000) 401-14

J. Bussell, 'Great Expectations: Can Maternity Coaching affect the Retention of Professional Women?', *International Journal of Evidence Based Coaching and Mentoring* 2 (2008): 14-26

S. A. Haddock, Scott J. Ziemba, T. S. Zimmerman and L. R. Current, 'Ten adaptive strategies for family and work balance: advice from successful families', *Journal of Marital and Family Therapy* 27 (2001): 445-58

Tom Hodgkinson, *The Idle Parent: Why Less Means More When Raising Kids* (Penguin, 2010)

Averil Leimon, François Moscovici and Helen Goodier, *Coaching Women to Lead* (Routledge, 2010)

Libby Purves, *How Not to Be a Perfect Mother* (Thorsons, 2004)

Working Better – Fathers, family and work report from the Equality and Human Rights Commission retrieved on 30/9/10: www.equalityhumanrights.com/news/2009/october/fathers-struggling-to-balance-work-and-family

www.rockchoir.com

www.popdance.co.uk

RESOURCES

Home-Start

Through a network of nearly 16,000 trained parent volunteers, Home-Start supports thousands of parents who are struggling to cope. www.home-start.org.uk and 0800 068 6368

Mumsnet

For parenting advice, campaigns and forums
www.mumsnet.com

National Childbirth Trust

Antenatal classes, nearly sales, childbirth advice
www.nct.org.uk

Netmums

For what's on in your area for families, advice and mums'
talk boards www.netmums.com

Index

asking for help 111, 114–15
asking for what you want
57–62
au pairs 140–2

boundaries, work–home
82–8, 258–9
breastfeeding 170–1,
220–1
British Household Panel
Survey 11

change, adapting to 230–2,
238–9
changing jobs 25–8
childcare
au pairs 140–2
childminders 125–30,
147–8
evaluating your options
123–5, 146–9, 212,
215–16
family and friends 110–
17, 142–5
nannies 130–4, 148
nurseries 134–40, 148–9
resolving issues 149–54

settling in period 90–1,
152–3, 216, 220, 224
and sickness 41, 133–4,
150–2, 175, 221
Childcare Link 129
Childminders 125–30,
147–8
children
and domestic chores
117–19, 175–6, 195,
197
entertaining 250–1
and parties 204
chores see domestic
chores
cleaners 192–5, 222
clothes for work 218–19,
225
coaches 257–8
colleagues 62–3, 78, 83–4,
90, 215, 218
commuting 228, 263
confidence 52–6, 223
Criminal Records Bureau
(CRB) 131

dads see partners

depression 32, 39–40, 188–9, 249
diaries 213, 250, 267
domestic chores
  cleaners 192–5, 222
  cooking 200–4, 222
  food shopping 198–9, 224
  good enough mindset 187–92, 216–17
  involving children in 117–19, 175–6, 195, 197
  laundry 196–8, 225

emotional support 112–13, 244–5
employers
  and flexible working 73–5
  maintaining contact with 63–9, 214, 217–18
energy levels 261–2
entertaining 203–4
equality see sexual equality
exercises
  advanced planning 229
  choosing childcare 146, 149
  do you need to renegotiate your role? 72–3
  easing yourself back into work 91–2
  getting a grip on your guilt 181–2
  how you can live the good enough mindset 191–2
  motherhood–work parallels 56–7
  my feelings about work 20–1
  what do you expect from yourself? 99–100
  your thrive audit 252–4
  your thrive manifesto 264
  your work–home boundaries 87–8

family and friends
  as childcare providers 142–5
  support networks 110–19, 219
Family Information Service 129
family life
  keeping it simple 250–2
  mealtimes 202–4, 245–6
  strategies for success 239
  team work 97–9
  weekend activities 246–8
family planner 106–7
fathers see partners
Female Brain, The 113–14, 164
financial independence 10–12 see also pay
first day at work 227–9

first weekend 229–30
flexible working
　employer's attitude to
　　73–5
　health benefits 74
　legislation 79–82
　steps for achieving 76–9
food shopping 198–9, 224
freedom 14–15 *see also* me
　time
friends *see* family and
　friends
full-time work 29–31

gender equality *see* sexual
　equality
government policies 39
grandparents 111, 112,
　143, 144–5
grocery shopping 198–9,
　224
guilt
　childcare arrangements
　　172–4
　child's illness 174–5
　domestic responsibilities
　　175–6
　lack of quality time 168–
　　70
　less commitment to work
　　177
　missing milestones
　　171–2
　not being a stay-at-home
　　mum 176

not having me time 179–
　80
positive and negative
　aspects 163
relationship with partner
　177–8
reliance on family support
　179
separation from children
　164–8
socially constructed
　160–2
stopping breastfeeding
　170–1
top ten techniques for
　managing 180–2

'have it all' debate 5–7
health and wellbeing 9–10,
　31–2, 74, 76, 219 *see
　also* depression
help, asking for 111, 114–
　15
hobbies 215, 240 *see also*
　me time
holiday allowance 89–90
holidays 244
Home-Start 273
housework *see* domestic
　chores

identity 12–14, 166
Idle Parent, The 250–1
illness and childcare 41,
　133–4, 150–2, 175, 221

internet resources *see*
online resources
internet shopping 199
ironing 196–7

job satisfaction 255–6

Keep In Touch days (KIT)
63–7, 214, 217–18

Laundry 196–8, 225
lunch breaks 261–2

mantras
Do What It Takes to Thrive
235–65
Find Childcare That Fits
Your Family 121–55
Get a Grip on Guilt 157–
83
Go for 'Good Enough' at
Home 185–207
Keep in Touch and Ask
for What You Want
49–93
Know Your Ideal Work
Scenario 1–47
Prepare for a Smooth
Return 209–33
See Your Family as a Team
95–120
maternity leave
legal requirements 40,
66, 71–2, 214

working during 42–3,
52–3, 63–7, 217–18
me time 239–43, 263
mealtimes 202–4, 245–6
mental stimulation 3–4,
15–16
mentors 256–8
money 10–12 *see also* pay
motivation for returning to
work
contribution to society 20
freedom 14–15
health benefits 9–10
identity 12–14
maintaining skills 16–17
mental stimulation 3–4,
15–16
money 10–12
mothers' views 7–9
role models 18–19
Mumsnet 201, 202

nannies 130–4, 148
Nanny Tax 131
National Childbirth Trust
(NCT) 3–4, 51, 171
Netmums 30
nurseries 134–40, 148–9

Ofsted 125, 129, 130, 131,
135, 146, 198, 215–16
Oliver, Jamie 202
online resources
breastfeeding 171

childcare 129, 131, 142
family planner 107
flexible working 38, 42
Home-Start 273
Mothers Work! 267
Mumsnet 201, 202
Netmums 30
self-employment 24, 25
online shopping 199

parenting buddies 218
*Parent's Guide to Choosing
    Childcare, The* 129
part-time work
benefits 31–3, 34–6
pay penalties 17–18, 30
quality part-time roles
    36–40
partners
as childcare providers
    142–3, 246–7
communicating with
    100–2, 245
and equality 33–4, 98,
    102–5
maintaining relationship
    244–5
opposition to working
    mothers 108–10
resentment of 107–8
pay
moving from full-time to
    part-time 17–18, 30
negotiating 58–62, 255

peer pressure 21–3, 181
permataining 250–1
postnatal depression 112,
    162, 249
preparation for return to
    work
adapting to change 230–
    2, 238–9
to-do lists 213
three to six months before
    214–17
one month before
    217–22
one week before 222–5
one day before 225–7
first day back 227–9
first weekend 229–30

reluctance to return to work
    44–6
resources *see* online
    resources
Robinson, Winifred 187–8,
    251
role models 18–19
role renegotiation
at home 98
at work 70–3

self-employment 23–5
self-esteem 11, 52–6,
    223
separation anxiety 41,
    167–8

settling in, childcare 90–1,
    152–3, 216, 220, 224
sexual equality
  and domestic chores 98,
    102–5, 188–9
  and work 33, 39, 58–9
Sheconomics 11, 195
sickness and childcare 41,
    133–4, 150–2, 175, 221
single mums 9, 51, 110,
    113, 115, 116
skills
  acquired through
      motherhood 55
  maintaining work 16–17
sleep 248–50
social life 203–4, 215, 219,
    225 *see also* me time
Statutory Maternity Leave
    see maternity leave
stay-at-home mums 5–6,
    161
support networks 110–19,
    219

team work (family) 97–9
*Time Management for Manic
    Mums* 224

Times Online Alpha Mummy
    Blog 36–7, 111
timing of return to work
    40–4
tiredness 248–50
to-do lists 213
*Transitions: Making Sense of
    Life's Changes* 230
travelling to and from work
    228, 263

washing clothes 197–8,
    225
weekend activities 246–8
well woman appointments
    219
What Women Want 44
Women Like Us xi, 38
work clothes 218–19,
    225
work-home boundaries
    82–8, 258–9
working life
  being focused and
      productive 259–60
  job satisfaction 255–6
  lunch breaks 261–2
Working Tax Credit 131

Jessica Chivers
the thinking woman's coach

If you would like to find out more about

'Women Returner' coaching programmes

*

Booking Jessica to speak or run a seminar

*

1:1 Coaching

Then visit

www.jessicachivers.com

For radio, TV and other media enquires email

hello@jessicachivers.com

Hay House Titles of Related Interest

The Manic Mum's Guide to Magnificent Parenting,
by Allison Mitchell

More To Life Than Shoes,
by Nadia Finer and Emily Nash

Time Management for Manic Mums,
by Allison Mitchell

Work It Out!,
by Des McCabe

ABOUT THE AUTHOR

Jessica Chivers is the Thinking Woman's Coach. She was *Look* magazine's first 'Life Consultant' columnist and is regularly on the radio and in print dishing out zesty comment to inspire women in magazines such as *SHE, Prima Baby* and *Top Santé*.

She has a first class psychology background and has been inspiring professional women to make smooth, successful changes as a coach, writer and speaker for seven years.

Jessica regularly coaches teams and individuals in companies such as Barclays, the BBC, M&S and Veolia, and specializes in helping organizations retain and manage the transition of maternity and paternity leavers back into the workplace. She leads a team of coaches in delivering innovative 'comeback' programmes and is passionate about mothers being able to combine meaningful work with family life – if they want to. Over the years she has helped a great many women kick-start their climb up the career ladder, shift into self-employment, and make a smooth return to work after children.

Jessica is also a Mind Gym and Parent Gym coach, who has been featured on BBC News.

She is married to Nick and they live in Hertfordshire with their two children, Monty and Artemis.

To find out more about any of Jessica's work or availability to help you, your organization or campaign see www.jessicachivers.com or email hello@jessicachivers.com

www.jessicachivers.com